Under the Banyan Tree

Ruby Anik

Under the Banyan Tree

Cover Design and Print book interior
Typeset by: Book Media Services:

www.bookmediaservices.com

FOREWORD

Once, a long time ago, as a new first-generation Indian American immigrant to the United States, when I was still learning to navigate two universes, I said to my father, "I don't feel like I belong anywhere! India is no longer home, and neither is the US!" My father has long been gone but his wisdom endures. In his customary optimistic manner, he said, "Why don't you think you have two homes! India where you grew up, will always be home and the US where you are growing up is now your chosen home!" Armed with that perspective I had permission to return to India as of right and flourish in my new chosen home.

When author Ruby Anik, a gifted and evocative writer, asked me to write a foreword to this brilliant collection of stories, I was humbled and honored. **_Under the Banyan Tree,_** is a collection of stories masterfully narrated by Ruby who captures the essence of us transplants from South Asia, longing to hang on to what we once knew, drawing strength from our foundations, and resolutely flourishing in our new home. Those readers who have known and loved both continents, will find shared experiences in these pages. The second-generation immigrants who only know the subcontinent through tales told by their elders will find a context for their own existence. And those who neither have a lived nor a familial connection to the subcontinent, will get an insight into the struggles and triumphs of people straddling multiple cultures.

In these pages, you will be delighted by stories like Vatsala's, who found Lord Shiva's Trishul in her backyard and Preeti's book that tells tales of shared immigrant experiences. Niloufer's neuroscience story validates the wisdom of a traditional cup of tea. You will be moved by the Dixits and Kathawallas who turned grief and adversity into meaning and purpose. Your heart strings will be tugged by Rijuta's story of becoming a fierce advocate for individuals with special needs. Sarla's tale epitomizes resilience, and the uninhibited Divya —self-expression. Experience India through the eyes of young Madan. Feel pride as you read about the accomplishments of Zarina, a celebrated Minnesotan; Aamera, the anti-racism and equity advocate and theater maker; Shehla, the citizen of humanity; Kumud, who embodies the essence of service to others; Prakash who was mentored by none other than Mother Teresa; Asgi, whose scientific achievements have impacted so many; Santosh, the epitome of grit and perseverance; the roar of Jyotiee's entrepreneurial spirit; and Jeevan and Akhil, young people up to big things. It is heart-warming to read about *Hum*, where a community creates space for seniors to forge new friendships. In "Soul Curry," you will find a collection within a collection of powerful short stories. What all these stories have in common is a connection to where we come from, the fortitude with which we have adapted, and the incredible difference we are making in our communities.

Under the Banyan Tree, a beautiful and meaningful title. To quote Ruby, "the Banyan Tree has taken on significance as a symbol of fertility, life, and resurrection." The Banyan Tree conjures up imagery of a place central to a community, where elders impart wisdom, and generational stories are handed down. Just like being under that Banyan tree back home, the reader of this wonderful collection of stories will be enriched as they turn the pages and discover that Ruby has drawn them in, filling them with pride and warm nostalgia!

— Savita Harjani, Esq.
Author of Postcards from Within:
Random Ramblings of an Ordinary Human
Recipient of IPPY, NIEA, & Reader Views
literary awards

CHAPTERS

The 'Roar' of the Muddy Tiger 9

Divya Maiya: Front and Center 16

A Lotus Blooms 24

Jeevan-Teen On The Go 37

Citizen of Humanity 45

Theater-Maker 56

Madan's Travel Journal 67

Giving back where needed 77

Soul Curry 87

A Lifetime of 'Seva' 111

This Grandma Is Unbelievable 118

Curious! Collaborative! Highly
Motivated! 124

Good Will Ambassador 131

My Little Fighter 144

YUM YUM YUM 152

"I'm paid to go fishing everyday..." 168

How My Nervous System Became My
Cup Of Tea 174

'One doesn't need feet, but courage to fly
high' 184

Seven Rivers to Ten Thousand Lakes .. 191

Gardens: Inspiration and Remembrance
.... 198

Please visit *DesiStoriesAshaUSA.com* or scan the QR code to enjoy more photographs in vivid color

Under the Banyan Tree

CHAPTER 1

THE 'ROAR' OF THE MUDDY TIGER

Jyotiee Kistner is an entrepreneur and restaurateur. Her food venture, Muddy Tiger bistro, serves Indian street food with a Maharashtrian twist.

Jyotiee grew up in Pune, helping and learning from her father, who ran a food business catering to the cycle of weddings, birthdays, religious and social events that form the entertainment fabric of life in India.

She migrated to the US in 2011 to pursue her career in the software industry. Traveling around the US for work, she found dense hubs of Indians and Indian restaurants, but the cuisine inevitably focused on the ubiquitous butter chicken and Naan, a general euphemism for Indian cuisine in the US, especially Minnesota.

Under the Banyan Tree

Until 2018, Jyotiee continued to excel as a
software designer, eventually being introduced
by a friend to her now husband, Andy Kistner.
Their visit to the city of Jyotee's youth, Pune,
was a culinary delight for Andy. *"It was a feast
for my husband. He was really surprised with
all the food and culture"*.
Flavors of authentic Indian cuisine vastly
differ, sometimes in every town and village in
India, and they saw an opportunity to present
something different.

*"In India, each region has their own specialty.
It is not stereotypical [Indian-American] food.
Language and food is so different every 100
kilometers in India. While some regions serve
hot and spicy dishes, others specialize in more
sweet and savory meals"*. In Pune, Marathi
cuisine is the *specialty*. *"My [native] city has a
balance of sweet, spicy, tangy [and]
sometimes bitter—everything in one dish. We
wanted to share what Western India is doing,
and especially Indian street food."*

Indian street food, or chaat, is essentially
quick, accessible and affordable bites. Rather
than sitting down, customers order food from a
food stall and grab it on the go. It's the food
locals eat on a daily basis. *"At home, chaat is
affordable for any economic level,"* Jyotiee
says. The people selling the food make
everything fresh daily and she wanted to take a
similar approach.

Under the Banyan Tree

To introduce Marathi cuisine to Twin Cities residents, the couple opened a food tent in 2018 that made appearances at the Centennial Lakes Farmers Market. They also experimented with restaurant pop ups at the Minneapolis Shake Shack, run by her restaurant mentors, in the process learning how to run a commercial kitchen. Growing in popularity, they opened a food truck in 2021, and in early 2023, they opened the Muddy Tiger Bistro featuring counter service in Edina.

Jyotiee and Andy Kistner: Photo Courtesy of Edina Magazine

Andy came up with the name Muddy Tiger, an unusual, catchy name for the business. The name resonated with Jyotiee, as she used to work for Save the Tiger Project with WWF-India. *"When we are in college, most students get involved with the [Tiger] Project through our education system,"* she says. Tigers are the national animal of India, and symbolize strength, speed, agility and grace, criteria she wanted to associate the restaurant with: *"Somehow today, I am still fascinated by the tiger. [Muddy Tiger] stays with people."*

Sweet, Tangy and Spicy

Specializing in the Marathi cuisine of that eponymous state, the contemporary, blue hued bistro dives into the snacks arena of 'chaat' and 'street food', recognized for its complexity of flavors and tangy essence, augmented by rice bowls and wraps. Special meals such as a vegetarian 'thali' or plate, feature dishes of textual depth, complexity and diverse flavors, including a soft puri with a hint of crispness for scooping up savory offerings.

Jyotiee embraces the sweet and spicy flavors from her hometown that have delighted the palate of both the informed and uninformed customers of her cuisine. The dishes use minimal spices and incorporate hometown ingredients such as coconut and peanuts. They can find a variety of vegetarian options, though chicken and lamb feature on her menu. The 'Tawa' chicken has become a customer favorite, and a safe way to sample the flavors of Marathi cuisine in a familiar format. Exploration and more adventurous eating usually follow!

Jyotiee says *"It just balances out that taste of everything in one bite,"* noting that there are no artificial flavors or preservatives in any of their dishes.
She has her unique blend of spices flown in from her hometown every three months or so. Her parents prepare the spice mix and send it

over in bulk to use in the restaurant. *"My dad used to have a catering business. I grew up helping him and learning from him, so all those recipes I grew up learning are from my home. All are family recipes."*

Jyotiee often has to explain to visitors that Muddy Tiger does not feature stereotypical Indian items such as curry and buttered chicken. She says these items are not served in her native city unless it's at North Indian themed restaurants.

Popular items at Muddy Tiger include Sabudana Vada (soft, savory and mildly sweet patty featuring tapioca, potatoes, peanuts, spices and herbs), Pav Bhaji (buttered and grilled buns with a delicately spiced lentil filling), Tawa Chicken, and Rose Falooda (layered dessert in the mold of a parfait or sundae). Vada Pav, one of Muddy Tiger's specialties, generates an explosion of soft and crunchy accents all within one bite.

The restaurant also adds occasional specials to its menu, featuring other regions in India, often in line with festivals and holidays such as Valentine's Day.

As a tribute to the Kistner's hard work, and countless hours poured into their 'labor of love', the press coverage has been gratifying. They have been featured in both Edina Magazine and MSP magazine and in 'EATER' Twin Cities on the South Asian Food Scene, and the 15 Hottest New Restaurants in the Twin Cities.

The Roar continues

The name 'Muddy Tiger' is memorable, and the authenticity of the tasty cuisine is ensuring return customers. *"All my dishes are really close to [the] original experience. Many people keep telling me, 'I used to eat this back home', and this is what makes the late nights and early mornings worth it. Me and my husband do everything from cooking to mopping the floors. We built the whole restaurant by ourselves. Whatever we have, we are putting in the restaurant,"* she says.

Jyotiee's ultimate goal is to bring her hometown to her Minnesota customers, so people can *"feel like they're home."* As evidenced by the press coverage and return customers, her goal is coming to fruition and Muddy Tiger continues to thrive.

CHAPTER 2

DIVYA MAIYA: FRONT AND CENTER

D ivya Maiya is the co-founder and CEO of SAATH (South Asian Arts and Theater House). Divya has brought positive attention to Minnesota's vibrant Indian community by using Bollywood dance to connect people, and raise awareness for social causes.

Divya grew up in Bangalore, dancing recreationally as a child, and transitioned to exploring different forms of dance once she was in college. Grad School brought her to the US in 2009, and while at the University of Wisconsin, Madison she competed nationally on a college dance team. She moved to Minneapolis two years later to join her husband, and while her day job at Best Buy utilizes her technical skills, her passion for dance has moved to center stage.

Divya glows when she is noticed, when her dances cause disruption and flurry, always clad in vibrant and colorful costumes.

Divya uses dance deliberately to create her own community. In 2012, Divya and two friends approached Tapestry Folk dance center about offering a weekly 'drop-in' class: 'Bollywood Dance Scene', which soon became the most popular offering at Tapestry. The group started performing around town, and charged a small fee to cover expenses for their weekly dance programs. Dance sessions were devoted to one routine, from introduction to performance, and open to both beginners and dancers at all skill levels, offering a new experience at each session.

As Divya says *"Bollywood dance is inspired by various dance forms like classical, folk, as well as street dances. So it's a huge mash-up of those forms along with hip-hop, belly dancing and jazz. People of all age groups can dance together. It is over the top ridiculous, and you need that to forget all the serious and grim happenings in your life. It is loud and colorful; just what Minnesota needs especially in winters"*.

Since its founding, the Bollywood dance scene has strived to advance cultural and social understanding. Divya has organized dance  flash mobs in celebration of India's Independence Day and on the frozen Minnesota lakes. Divya and her friends gathered on a pristine white field, pouring their hearts into dance, drawing attention to the beauty of a cold February day in Minnesota. As Divya recalls, *"It was a very beautiful day, and many people showed up."* With the combination of vibrant color and loud, pulsating music, the dancer's storytelling captured the passers-by.

The company's mission is to bring awareness to social causes through dance, and have organized the 'One Billion Rising to End Violence Against Women' event to end violence against women and girls.

They have also partnered with 'Out in The Backyard', a group that helps the LGBTQ community to counter isolation. This resulted in a bi-weekly program teaching Bollywood dance to promote health and wellness for the LGBTQ community, and bridge the gap between community and non-community members.

Their latest production in September 2023, 'AKS – Acceptance, Kindness, Support' was about 'reflection', a show about self-discovery and resilience, continuing to support the LGBTQ community. A diverse cast of 70+ people presented a 3-act story to celebrate trans joy – the delight of living authentically.

Bollywood Dance Scene has evolved and is now known as 'South Asian Arts and Theater House', or SAATH, which means 'togetherness' or 'companionship' in Hindi and other Indian languages. Divya says she wanted a company that would be welcoming to all. *"You find fewer opportunities for adults to perform, and this type of dance is energizing";* her goal is to provide a *"center place"* where a diverse group of amateur dancers can enjoy themselves and let loose their creativity.

Since its founding, SAATH has put on shows at the Minnesota Fringe Festival where they were the top selling show in 2014, 2015 and 2016 before starting their own festival 'MinneUtsav'. *"We've done this on a shoestring,"* says Divya.

Under the Banyan Tree

"From tech to songs, it just kind of flowed."
These shows are available for viewing on the
SAATH website at *https://SAATHmn.org*

**'Hi Hello Namaste' in 2014 on following
your dreams;**

**'Spicy Masala Chai' in 2015 on the
issues of love in all forms including
LGBTQ relationships ;**

**'Bezubaan: The Voiceless' in 2016 on the
issue of Islamophobia;**

**'Love You Zindagi' in 2017 on the issue
of mental awareness especially in the
South Indian Community;**

**'The land of Maaya' in 2018 on the
issues of disability and ableism;**

**'Home Sweet Ghar' in 2019 on the issue
of home and creating a home after
moving to a new country;**

**Desi Heart Crust' exploring the
relationship of a black and Indian
couple through the lens of race, culture
and activism.**

"I'm all about bringing people together", Divya
passionately states, *"and dance is one way I
know how to do that"*.

SAATH has continued to teach dance since 2012, and the joy that Bollywood dancing elicits draws the wider public to her weekly 'drop-in' dance classes held on Thursday nights. They are inclusive, and welcome folks of every gender, identity and race. There are returning dancers who know each other, the music, and the dance moves well, and newcomers who are made to feel a core part of the group. On average, there are 25 attendees who exuberantly respond to the vibrant music and choreography of the South Asian continent.

Divya draws from a pool of about 20 choreographers who keep the classes fresh using different styles, language, dance movements and music.

At her classes, Divya's sparkle shines through her exertions, and her spirited assessment, that SAATH and performance is *"less about the audience, and more about the people in the community of dance, and the classes"* is on the mark!

The social ecosystem Divya wanted to build for herself and for her community through dance, is alive and well! And that, she says, *"feels like home."*

Divya's love of adventure combined with her desire to constantly do something unique has resulted in a broad social media following. Her exploits of skiing in a 'sari' have gained her positive notoriety.

After practicing the sport not just in a sari, but also skirts, suits and lehengas, she has become a mini celebrity on the internet with many of her videos going viral and garnering millions of viewers.

And they also have another purpose close to Divya's heart, *"I see these videos being extremely empowering for myself and a lot of women"*. She also finds it *"liberating"* to see that people were motivated by witnessing a brown woman participating in sports, wearing a non-traditional outfit like a sari.

Divya's skiing in a sari is captured in a short video through the YouTube link:

https://youtu.be/ytCyQ4mTTpM?si=TEL5h9 wY-w5JweYm

Under the Banyan Tree

Divya aptly captures who she is, *"As a sportswoman and a dancer performer, this feels like these two worlds were coming together. This combination of adrenaline and pride is what I thrive on"*.

Divya's own words sum her up perfectly:

"I'm a very confident person. I don't have inhibitions. [When I was little], they kept putting me in the back row, or gave me boy's parts because I had short hair. I'm not doing that. I'm not staying in the corner. **I want to be front and center"**.

CHAPTER 3

A LOTUS BLOOMS

Two inspiring foundations set up by families who have experienced tragedy, and created a meaningful difference from their grief are featured in 'A Lotus Blooms'.

Coping with the loss of a loved one is something no family should ever have to go through. As the Lotus flower symbolizes purity, overcoming adversity and rebirth, the Dixit's **('shreyadixit.org')** and the Kathawalla's (**'Zaharakathawalla.org**') have set up foundations that in different yet similar ways are celebrating their daughter's lives, making a difference to the lives of others and helping them cope with their loss.

Shreyadixit.org

SHREYA

Killed November 1, 2007
at age 19

Would still be alive today
but for an irresponsible
act of a distracted driver

Let's End Distracted Driving & Save Lives

Shreya Dixit, a sophomore at the University of Wisconsin, Madison was coming home to spend an early Diwali with her family in Minnesota. She was in the front passenger seat, when the driver in a split second of distraction crashed the car into a concrete pylon. Though the other 3 occupants of the car survived, Shreya was killed instantly, plunging the family into grief.

Vijay Dixit, Shreya's father, traded his professional career for social advocacy after the distracted driver killed his 19 year old daughter on November 1, 2007. Vijay and his wife Rekha and their surviving daughter Nayha established the Shreya R. Dixit Memorial Foundation, *http://www.shreyadixit.org*, a non-profit with the mission to transform the driving culture in the nation.

The mission of the foundation is to ***Educate*** (through Vijay's Book 'One Split Second', establish Distraction-Free Life Clubs, Podcasts and Driver-Ed scholarships); *Take Action* (annual Raksha 5k Walk, endow internships, blogging, create audio-visual productions and safety messaging campaigns); and support *The Shreya Innovation Lab* (the EyeDA product: a technology device targeting distracted driving behaviors with proactive visual and audio alerts for the driver).

A key target audience of the foundation is teens and young adults, and the goal is to engage them with a three pronged approach:

Education: The Foundation's education material and tools train youngsters to become peer advocates capable of influencing their peers to adopt distraction-free driving behaviors.

Incentives: The Foundation uses meaningful non-financial (for the last 3 years, members of the Distraction-Free Life Club have been awarded the Emerging Leaders Award from the Department of Public Safety) and financial incentives to promote responsible driving behaviors. The foundation donates about $25k to $30k a year and grants include 12-15 $300 scholarships towards driver education training on a yearly basis; paid summer internships with about 50 beneficiaries in the past four years from all over the US; $2500 for 5 students to attend a boot camp at the Northern

Film Alliance, an organization that teaches teens and youth how to make films and provides audio-visual coaching.

Actions: Education and Incentives valued by the youth and funded by the foundation, inspire teens to execute innovative projects and showcase their creations with pride at public events:

EyeDA

An important project that the foundation is sponsoring with 15 current and former Eden Prairie HS students (mentored by experts in Machine and Artificial Language) from the foundation's 'Distraction-Free Life Club is **EyeDA**. This project was kicked off last year and is in Phase 2 of its development, and expects to go to market in the near future.

EyeDA targets distracted driving behaviors with proactive visual and audio alerts through an innovative rearview mirror device. The target for this device is large corporations, fleet operations, State agencies and individual consumers, and will serve as a useful training tool for driver-ed programs.

This link connects to a short news story from WCCO-CBS Minnesota reports on EyeDA. *https://youtu.be/JGukRSRIzTQ*

Passage of the Hands Free Bill

The hands-free bill was signed by the Governor of Minnesota and went into effect in 2019. Though hands-free is not necessarily distraction-free, it was a big step forward, since the driver can use a cell phone only by voice commands, without holding it. Vijay was a tireless advocate for the bill's passage, lobbying the Governor's office, Departments of Public Safety, Transportation, and the Minnesota Safety Council amongst many others.

Speaking Engagements

The foundation participates in planned speaking engagements which have included a Round Table hosted by Cargill Corporation at their HQ, with Senator Amy Klobuchar as the keynote speaker; Vijay Dixit's TedX Talk in October 2021: *https://youtu.be/BuCOWJu2IwU?si=vYtGGF V2FauOwwRP*; the 26th Annual Michigan Traffic Safety Summit in June 2023; and the upcoming 2023 Minnesota Toward Zero Deaths Conference in November 2023.

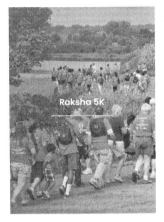

Raksha Walk

The Foundation's annual Raksha Walk is key to their fundraising activities and keeping the foundation's mission alive in the hearts and minds of participants, sponsors and legislators. Since the inception of the Raksha Walk in 2009, all Minnesota Governors have proclaimed the day of the Minnesota walk as Distraction-Free Driving Awareness Day in the state of Minnesota.

The walk is named after the Indian Festival 'Raksha Bandhan' that commemorates a centuries-old tradition in which a sister ties a ceremonial band on her brother's wrist creating an inseparable bond. The goal of the walk is to encourage a similar bond between drivers on the road, promising to drive distraction-free, to protect each other and the community.

The event is also poignant since the location of the walk, Purgatory Creek Park is a war memorial in Eden Prairie, MN and a gazebo at the location, is covered with photos of those lost to distracted driving.
In addition to the walk in MN, two parallel walks also occur in San Francisco and New

Jersey organized by friends of the family.
KARE-11 NBC's brief news story has
highlighted 2022's Raksha Walk.
https://youtu.be/PYWEb4vUhCE

Celebrating Shreya

Shreya's story will continue to change the lives
of countless others through the efforts of her
family and the work of her foundation.
As an organ donor, Shreya helped save more
lives.
Shreya was also a talented musician, a soprano,
the only 6th grader in the High School Choir,
who also sang with the Minnesota Youth Choir,
and trained one on one with 'Oksana Bryn', a
faculty member of the MacPhail Center of
music.

"Music was her energy"

A moving tribute to what Shreya's unfinished
story might have been, is poignantly rendered
in the YouTube video:
https://youtu.be/5Zod5W8_um4

Zaharakathawalla.org

Zahara Kathawalla, a vibrant, loving and determined 23 year old woman was a proud graduate of the Blake School and the School of Business at the University of Wisconsin-Madison. After her graduation, she moved to Kansas City to work for Cargill as a Commodity Merchant Associate.

Zahara was tragically killed by a racing car in a hit-and-run, while she was crossing the street with a friend on June 21, 2020 in Kansas City.

The Zahara Kathawalla (ZKF) foundation was established by her parents Salim and Farida Kathawalla to honor the memory of their daughter Zahara, 'who shone her light, positivity, and love on everyone she met during her 23-year earthly journey'.

About Zahara

Zahara mastered the ability to live each day with intention, curiosity and infectious joy. She triumphed over her childhood shyness and was known for her ability to talk to anyone. While at UW-Madison, she led adventure-based leadership and team building workshops. She had a zest for travel and visited nearly 40 Countries. Travel was not just about the sites, but experiencing the culture in its most authentic form and turning strangers into friends. *"I also travel to learn about my community, history and society. Traveling makes me feel whole"*.

She took mindful eating seriously, savoring each bite of dessert, especially her favorites: ice cream and chocolate lava cakes. Zahara enjoyed listening to music, especially loved how music connected to her emotions.

Zahara became involved in volunteering and community service from a young age. During High School, she volunteered at LearningWorks, a program to help Minneapolis public school students prep for college, and in Kansas City at Cornerstones for Cares as a youth mentor. She had also joined the Kansas City Chapter of the Scholarship Committee and Board of Directors of the University of

Wisconsin Alumni Association.
Zahara resonated with the idea that *"education is key"*.

Zahara was a loving and grateful daughter, supportive sister, commodities trader, world traveler, music aficionado, yogi and joyful friend!

About The Zahara Kathawalla Foundation

The Zahara Kathawalla Foundation (ZKF) *http://www.zaharakathawalla.org*, was established to support young adults, who do not have the means to pursue Zahara's passions for personal betterment.

The mission of the ZKF is to award 'need-based' funding that supports young individuals on their path towards personal growth, through experiences and opportunities in education, cultural exploration and wellness.
The mission supports the foundation's vision of 'A world where people have the opportunity to pursue their passion and live life to the fullest'.

Three areas of focus support a theory of positive change:
1. Educational opportunities enable passionate, dedicated, curious and empowered citizens.
2. Cultural Exploration through travel lends itself to an expanded awareness, outlook and

acceptance of people everywhere.
3. Well-being is the foundation for life balance, happiness, mindfulness, relationships and growth.

Over the last three years, the ZKF has raised over $100,000 and donated close to $20,000, towards the foundation's pillars of Education, Cultural Exploration and Wellness.
Organizations and Individuals that have benefited include: Be That Neighbor, University of Wisconsin Madison Business School, Al-Zahra Madrasah, the Blake School and Park Nicollett's NOW Telehealth Mental Health Program.
Grants are approved against a list of criteria that connect to the ZKF mission and pillars, connection to Zahara and the impact of the grant on an individual person.

The logo for the ZKF is a stylized version of a sunflower. Since Zahara was a junior in HS, she loved sunflowers. It was designed over a 6 month period by a family friend of the Kathawallas.

Z5K Fun Run

For the past three years the Z5K Fun Run has served to bring over 400 people together virtually (on a global basis), and in person (Gold Medal Park on the Mississippi River and

Lake Harriet) to commemorate Zahara's life and raise money for the foundation. The run/walk kicks off with Yoga and dance in honor of Zahara's daily 5.30am sessions, and concludes with music and food where participants celebrate the day.

Remembering Zahara

Zahara is best remembered by savoring each day; each bite of something indulgent; and each moment of laughter with music. Her mindfulness, thoughtfulness, and one-of-a-kind joys are just some of the hallmarks of her legacy.

At age 13 , Zahara wrote a letter to her high school self where she said: *"Thinking into the future on who I want to be before I die, [that] would be, make a GREAT impact on everyone else [and] being remembered as an honest, fun, trusting friend anyone can count on"*.

In her 23 years, Zahara definitely accomplished this goal.

Celebrating Zahara

Zahara enjoying her favorite breakfast of Avocado Toast at a friend's home on June 20, 2020. Zahara lost her life the next day on June 21, 2020

If you wish to support the work of these stellar organizations, a link to Donate can be found on their websites.

CHAPTER 4

JEEVAN-TEEN ON THE GO

Jeevan Venkatesan is a young man extraordinaire!

He is a sophomore at Penn State University

Park, majoring in Aerospace Engineering. He explores the world by volunteering, diving into cultural experiences, internships and entrepreneurial ventures. His smile lights up his face, as he enthusiastically recounts his many achievements. At the same time, genuine humility and charm radiate to win over the listener. His zest for life and go go attitude seem difficult to sustain, but like the 'energizer bunny', he has been forging ahead since he took his first steps, enthusiastically supported by his parents, Priya and Venky.

The first sign of future promise came at the age of 4, with his story published in the Hindu Mandir newsletter 'Voice of Mandir' in 2008. And the promise continued to unfold as the years went by, in the arenas of Music, Sports, Volunteerism, Internships and Academics as detailed below.

Music and Dance

Expressing himself is critical to Jeevan, using all forms of dance and music, including Bhangra and Bollywood. He has been involved with the 'South Asian Arts and Theater House (SAATH)': *https://www.Saathmn.org*, for the past 10 years, a non-profit that establishes a cohesive community through dance.

He founded 'Dance for a Cause: 2019-2021', raising money by teaching dance and donating to local organizations; and co-founded 'Bhangra Thrills', a professional dance group that dances around the Twin Cities. He also participated in Twin Cities Euphoria, dancing at Jazba 2022 (*https://www.jazbamn.com*), a Bollywood-fusion dance competition set up to raise funds for 'Women in Need/WIN'.

Jeevan has played Violin since he was three, and was in the Greater Twin Cities Youth Symphonies for two years (GTCYS). He was

First Chair leading his section for one year, playing all around the Twin Cities including Orchestra Hall and Ted Mann Hall.

Sports

In addition to his cultural pursuits, Jeevan has played many sports since he was 5, including

Cricket for Team Minnesota, Basketball for school teams, Golf, Sailing in summer and Bowling for which he received two varsity letters in the 10th and 12th grade.
A favorite is chess, which he has played in, and won, many tournaments.

Volunteerism and Internships

Volunteering has been a key part of Jeevan giving back to his community.
He led the Social Media efforts and website for the Maple Grove Rotary Club, actively working their community events. Passionate about climate change, he has volunteered with Earth Uprising, a global, youth-led climate movement.
One of his formative experiences was the 'Eagle UA 5 day camp focusing on leadership, entrepreneurship and innovation.

He also worked with the India Association of Minnesota (IAM) since 2019 as Head Photographer, Oral history intern, India Fest, Golf Events, Marketing Programs and handled logistics for Corporate Connect in 2019.

With IAM as a sponsor, Jeevan apprenticed with the 'Seeds to Harvest' organization on an entrepreneurial venture for 'A Better Community Impact' fellowship in 2020-2021. He was one of 100 High Schoolers (HS) who were guided through the field of entrepreneurship and business creation. He was the last HS left after eliminations to present his concept G-BOX to the Mayor of Minneapolis.

The concept was a fully biodegradable garbage can for parks, businesses and the community using bamboo sticks and coconut strings. Though the concept did not eventually move forward, Jeevan learnt valuable lessons on managing a business and success and failure.

First Prototype of G-Box, an entrepreneurial venture showcased at St. Paul event

St. Thomas Military Academy

Jeevan completed his formative HS education at St. Thomas Military Academy. His parents were seeking a structured organization that would provide discipline and diverse opportunities for extra curricular activities. The school certainly gave him that!

He participated in the Honor Guard all four years and provided services to the public on

Jeevan leading platoon march

behalf of the school at showcases and social events. He also participated in civil debates on worldview topics as part of the Lincoln Society for two years, and was a member of the Junior Varsity Math Team and Quiz Bowl.

He contributed to the school newspaper as photographer of school events and was a student ambassador for the school for two years.

He participated in the Model United Nations for two years; the Blue Origin Contest, tasked to develop a test that could be brought into Space; and the First Tech Challenge, building robots that got his team into the regionals in 2019.

An overarching theme being his interest in Aerospace

NASA Hunch

One of his most notable achievements was participating in the NASA HUNCH Design and Prototype program for 3+ years and as a finalist in 2020. The challenge was to develop a carbon fiber wheel for a lunar wagon, that could be potentially used in a real-

life NASA mission.
(*https://www.nasahunch.com*)

Though teams were invited for the final design review in Houston at Rocket Park on Johnson Space Center April 15, 2020, the COVID pandemic unfortunately prevailed.

As the summer of 2023 came to a close, and Jeevan wrapped up his summer jobs as Math Tutor and at retail food outlets, he has continued the clubs/experiences at Penn State University (PSU) that he began in his freshman year.

Production Manager with **PSU Jadhoom**, a Bollywood fusion dance team that competes on the DDN (Desi Dance Network) circuit; **PSU Formula1**, contributing ideas to help his team optimize aerodynamics with suspension and body ideas; The **PSU AVT (Advance Vehicle Team) club**, year 2 of 5 year program building a level 4 autonomous car, as a member of the system engineering team working on car system and safety features. The team has collectively placed 3rd in this year's competition and Jeevan's focused area (safety and system engineering) placed 1st; **AIAA Club** to gain better experience in the field of aerospace through speaker series and networking events.

Under the Banyan Tree

As Jeevan, at the tender age of 19, having
already achieved a lifetime's worth of
academic, business, cultural and community
credits, steps on the yet untrodden path of his
future, we say 'GO FOR IT!'

CHAPTER 5

CITIZEN OF HUMANITY

Shehla Mushtaq is a founding Chair and former Board Member of AshaUSA.

As a woman who has traveled the globe, Shehla identifies herself not only as a citizen of Minnesota, but as a citizen of humanity. 'No religion is greater than humanity'*, which sums up Shehla's character and the way she moves through life, to care for others in her community and in the world.

*Pakistani philanthropist and humanitarian: Abdul Sattar Edhi

A Citizen of the World

Shehla was raised in Pakistan and received her formative education at a Catholic Convent, St. Joseph High School. She has always cherished the time she spent there, recognizing the importance of values learned! Her global experience of other world religions such as Buddhism and Hinduism, having grown up in an overwhelmingly Muslim country, combined with the values from her Catholic school education, combine to make her who she is today.

At the age of 19, she arrived in the US to obtain her Bachelor's and Master's in Electrical Engineering at Texas Tech University in Lubbock. She was struck by the individualism she saw in the U.S., in comparison to the strong family and community values in Pakistan. After a societal tug of war between going back to Pakistan to get married or pursuing further academics in the US, she gave in to pressure and went back to Karachi.

She spent a few adventurous years working with her elder brother at 'Next Hardware Shop', that they jointly founded, driving all over Karachi to pick up ailing hardware and repair computers. Eventually, after getting married she returned to the US, and had her first child, a girl, shortly before the infamous Minnesota Halloween storm of 1991. Her three grown up children Saher, 32 a security consultant lives in London, Nadya 30, is a technical data analyst in Chicago, and Aadil 27, is a software

engineer living in the Twin Cities.

Shehla believes in, and promotes the power of **'Connecting'** and **'Serving'** at the most fundamental level...as a thinking and feeling human being. This is illustrated in the interconnected paths of her life story featured below: ***The Poet, Citizen of Humanity and Business Person.***

The Poet

Shehla's father was an author and journalist of some note, and studied at Columbia University in New York and the London School of Economics. He passed away in 1998, having published over fifteen books. In Karachi, he was also the editor of the English newspaper: The Morning News and contributed regularly as a columnist for another English periodical: 'Dawn' still in circulation in Pakistan.

Following in the footsteps of her father's literary achievements, Shehla is a poet and novelist of some note herself.

Her book of poems called ***Barsaat Ki Khushboo (The Smell Of Rain),*** has been published in two editions. (Shehla's second book ***Barsaat Kay Khanay*** is in English and features her favorite recipes inherited from her mother and friends, with a few of her own). Shehla uses 'Barsaat' as her alias, a reflection of her love for the rains. Growing up, she went to Bombay each year during the monsoons, to be one with the rain and rejuvenate herself with its cleansing power. Her book is available at _https://www.littlebookcompany.net/Barsaatk ikhushboo_.

Three of the poem's titles and stories are featured below.

Kaheen Dair Na Ho Ja Aye: ***(Don't let it be too late).*** This poem is about using the present moment to tie loose ends, especially with relationships. Do it now, or else time may pass and it may be too late. Connect with those with whom connection has been broken for whatever reason, especially loved ones

Woh Dost Bun Ja O: (Be your best friend). This poem is about getting to know yourself. We are constantly in search of that friend who understands us, the one we want to pour our heart out to and hang out with. Don't look too far and wide, the friend is right with you: learn to be your own best friend.

Idhar Ya Odhar: (Here or there): This poem is about the tussle between the pull of two homes. One where Shehla was born and spent the early years of her youth, and the other in the US where she has lived for almost 4 decades. Both are her homes, with their own charm.

Under the Banyan Tree

Shehla's poem on the Pandemic 'O Mankind', also featured in the book is translated from Urdu and can be visualized using the link below:

https://drive.google.com/file/d/1gugw3hCEgt oZioPwqzjElon_gCVSeTKF/view?ts=646a525 a&skip_itp2_check=true

O Mankind

Man asks me, are you upset with me?

(I say) Tell me, in every century, what haven't I done for you?

You have plundered my beautiful earth

In front of my very eyes you have chopped down trees

You uprooted trees and left my forests bare

Yes, I am upset with you!

With garbage you filled my blue seas

You polluted my environment with poisonous gases

Under the Banyan Tree

Yes, I am upset with you!

Showing no mercy, you slaughtered my poor
animals

You plucked the flowers from my beautiful
gardens

Yes, I am upset with you!

O Mankind, you have been given this one
chance

Recognize that this is the time to now mend
your ways!

Citizen of Humanity

The time Shehla spent working in the UK,
Mexico, Argentina and Venezuela contributed
to her growth as a citizen of humanity. She has
served on many Boards, a consistent theme:
the celebration of women; social enterprise;
and connecting humanity.

*Vice Chair: Honoring Women Worldwide;
Board Member: Women Leading in
Technology; Vice Chair: Shift (organization
provided support to those in mid-life work
transitions); Chair: AshaUSA; Founder
and Board Member: Karsaz (local arts and*

culture organization creating awareness of South Asian culture); **Board Co-Chair***: Social Enterprise MSP (https://socialenterprisemsp.org);* **President***: Interfaith Circle;* **Vice Chair***; Minnesota Multifaith Network*

She considers her most important contributions to have been in building connections, bridges and community, through conversations, dialog sessions and events.

Interfaith Circle

She is a founding member and President of Interfaith Circle which started out in Eden Prairie as an informal group in response to the unsettled environment after 9/11 (*https://interfaithcircle.wordpress.com*). Later, it was formalized and exists today as a program under the Eden Prairie Community Foundation, with structure and bylaws that are not under the umbrella of any specific faith organization.

Through the years, off and on, the organization has remained committed to promoting conversation and greater understanding of faiths, diversity and cultural differences. Multiple faiths: Christian, Muslim, Catholic, Hindu, Jewish, Native American and Baha'i are some of the many groups that have come together through Interfaith Circle's programming.

The signature event of the Interfaith Circle has been a celebration at Thanksgiving time. The different communities come together to read, dance and sing, highlighting their faith traditions during this celebratory event. Over the years, the event has drawn 100s of attendees, up to 1100 one year.

As Shehla says *"our goal is to ensure that the conversations between people in the community continue. We want people to embrace their differences and say: I want to have that conversation"*.

The Interfaith Circle was honored with a 2020 'Excellence' award for its documentary feature 'Becoming One: The Power of Our Stories' by the Best in the Midwest Media Fest. The goal was to spark more thoughtful and broader consideration of the challenges of living and working in an increasingly diverse Eden Prairie.

Minnesota Multifaith Network Council

More recently, Shehla has become involved on a State wide basis with the Minnesota Multifaith Network and serves as Vice Chair of the Network Council. The two main functions are 1. To convene interfaith leaders, faith organizations and practitioners across the state and 2. To communicate opportunities and resources for interfaith involvement and learning: *https://www.mnmultifaith.org/*

Humphrey School Fellows

Shehla also serves as a host family for the International Fellows program at the Humphrey School of Public Affairs at the University of Minnesota. She is in her tenth year of hosting these mid-career professionals, and has had Fellows from Lebanon, Sierra Leone, Libya, Bangladesh, Pakistan, Burkina Faso, Macedonia and Morocco. Her hostess skills backed by a love of all things culinary ensure successful gatherings at her home.

In 2020, she was one of 50 Minnesotans to be recognized for her work in the community. Shehla was awarded the 'Community Cultural Cooperator Award' from AARP Minnesota & Pollen's 50 over 50, celebrating hope, resilience and the outstanding contributions that make Minnesota a better place.

https://www.pollenmidwest.org/stories/2020-50-over-50/

Business Impact

Having lived in the US for 30+ years, Shehla has leveraged her IT and Business expertise with a variety of businesses such as NCS, Pearson Government Solutions, Vangent, Inc, General Dynamics and United Health Group.

Twice, Shehla was named a Technology All Star, recognized for Technology Excellence and Leadership by the National Women of Color in 2007 and 2012.

Six years ago, she entered into a business partnership called Collectivity and serves as its Chief Operations Officer. It is a consulting cooperative that helps non-profits and social impact organizations maximize their impact by making effective use of their people, processes and technology (*https://www.collectivity.coop*)
The work at Collectivity is rewarding for Shehla, as it brings many of her passions, both professional and personal, together in one place.

Connections

Shehla's love of travel has taken her to many countries. She visits Pakistan multiple times a year to see her mother and family, keeping 'all' her connections alive.

One of her favorite stories is the 'Connection' she made with a young Somali girl whom she interacted with on her way home from tennis one day. She greeted the family with the traditional Arabic greeting. The young Somali girl was taken aback to hear Shehla, a woman not wearing a hijab, saying this greeting. The little girl then proceeded to ply Shehla with questions, seeking to understand this difference. Shehla patiently answered all her queries, using the opportunity as a teaching moment: that religion can be practiced on the individual level, accepting different versions, while sharing common values of charity, kindness and compassion.

Her new young friend, satisfied with their discussion, walked away with a happy smile on her face.

Shehla often talks to young people about the Japanese philosophy of 'Ikigai'. It is a concept that brings together 'what we love', 'what we are good at', what we are paid for' and 'what the world needs'. That point of integration is called 'Ikigai', Our Reason For Being'.

Shehla is a seeker at heart and is currently studying the 13th century Poet 'Rumi's' Persian work 'Masnavi'. One of her favorite quotes from that poem is 'Let the beauty of what you love, be what you do'.

CHAPTER 6

THEATER-MAKER

Aamera Siddiqui, is a theater-maker whose pursuit for social justice has been the driving force in her life.

By the time Aamera was 13, she had lived in five countries on three continents. She was born in Dar es Salaam, Tanzania and her experiences as a global nomad, growing up amongst multiple cultures, political crises, religions and races led her down the natural path of pursuing anti-racism and equity, and where she is today, a social Justice 'Theater-Maker'.

A Peripatetic Childhood

Aamera's parents were from Amroha, Uttar Pradesh, a city known for its culture, poets and writers. They moved to Tanzania in 1963, where Aamera was born in 1968. Career opportunities caused the family to subsequently move to Zambia, where her father was the Dean of the English Department at the college in Lusaka. With the huge Indian community in Zambia, life was happy and wonderful, till spillover political upheaval from Uganda resulted in their having to move back to India temporarily.

Her father eventually enrolled in the PhD program at Syracuse university, and the family, sad to leave India, found themselves in the US, a difficult adjustment after the comfort and warmth of life in Africa and India. Life's unpleasant reality check included student housing, racism and lack of diversity. At only 71/2 years, Aamera found she was the only Indian student, after schooling that had included British, Zambian, Indian and South African students and teachers. Her home life reflected the stress and tension of adjusting to a new culture, and displaced and disoriented, she found herself asking *where do I belong?* A ray of light or 'raunak' as Aamera calls it, was brought into the home when her mother started an in-home day care service for the children of other international families. It felt more global and what Aamera was used to.

Her father's next job on a two year contract with USAID (United States Agency for International Development), moved the family to Yemen. Aamera felt right at home in the International School in Sana'a with students from 175 countries. With her family, she also traveled around the Middle East and South Asia.

Rising Social Consciousness

After Yemen, the family came back to Syracuse, where Aamera spent her HS years. As an immigrant in the US, Aamera found herself assimilating, shedding aspects of her identity and silencing her true self to navigate invisible and negative narratives that sought to define her through the lenses of anti-immigrant rhetoric, policies and Islamophobia. The discomfort zone was her own home, her in-home culture being very different from her out of home culture.

In High School, Aamera's friends were all involved in theater but Aamera found that she could not relate to the plays being produced such as 'Showboat' and 'Into the Woods'. They were not her stories or reflective of her experiences. This changed when she took a course in African American literature and felt right at home.

Though she was on a pre-Med track and got her Masters of Health Administration from Penn State, she knew the medical field was not for her after an internship in that arena. She got involved in International Associations, public speaking on subjects pertinent to International students, and writing essays on issues close to her heart.

Her own experiences and involvement drew her to wanting to change the situation for others who were also experiencing exclusion, under-representation and oppression in a white dominant system. She strongly believed that everyone has the right to experience their life from a place of belonging.

This led her eventually to jobs as a MultiCultural Education Coordinator at Rochester community college in 1991, and Diversity Director at the private Blake School in Minneapolis, where she developed programming designed to support underrepresented students and families, advanced strategic diversity plans and educational programs to raise awareness around equity, inclusion and more. She also worked with low income and first generation students in programs such as Upward Bound, and provided support services to students hoping to obtain a college degree.

In 2004, she became a qualified administrator for the Intercultural Development Inventory, an online survey to assess inter-cultural competence and provide profile results at both an individual and organizational level. This launched her career as an anti-racism and equity consultant while simultaneously pursuing theater on a parallel track.

Theater

Aamera first discovered her love of theater and acting in High School, having inherited her cultural genes from her mother's side of the family, that included poets, TV producers and actors.

After moving to the Twin Cities in 1996, Aamera spent almost a decade trying to find a place in the thriving theater scene. In all that time, she found no plays that reflected her or her experiences. Like many artists of color, the message was 'theater is not for people like you'. She continued to support herself as an anti-racism and equity consultant, but eventually co-founded her own theater company 'Exposed Brick Theater (EBT)', with her partner Suzy Messerole.

She knew nothing about starting a theater, only that the established convention and canon excluded many voices, artists and aesthetics. EBT is a marriage of Aamera's two passions: theater and social justice, and is dedicated to telling untold stories, centering omitted narratives and creating art at the intersection of identities.

Exposed Brick Theater's philosophy of following the story and playwright has resulted in their 17th premiere in 19 years. They are funded by grants from the National McKnight foundation, Metropolitan Arts Council, MN State Arts Board and co-productions with other theaters such as the Pillsbury theater.

(More information on the EBT is available on their website: *https://exposedbricktheatre.com*)

"I believe in the magic of theater. It has the potential to create empathy and understanding across divisions by allowing audiences to experience life through someone else's perspective – even perspectives we may disagree with. Theater also has the power to dismantle stereotypes by replacing them with narratives that challenge limited knowledge of a particular culture or community. For this reason, I am focused on holding theater spaces where underrepresented artists and communities feel at home and can create plays and performances that authentically reflect their narratives and experiences".

Aamera as Writer, Producer, Director, Actor

A sampling of plays that Aamera has either written, produced, directed or acted in:

The Trouble With Bill

A short 12 minute musical about the Civil Rights Infringements resulting from the Patriot

Act. In this play, Aamera played the role of a librarian who is desperately trying to document and preserve 'The Bill of Rights', before the US Government eliminates them in the name of Freedom.

American as Curry Pie

Aamera's autobiographical one woman show that premiered at the History Theater in Saint Paul in 2011. In this play, Aamera explored the challenges, humor and irony of straddling two

different cultures: her home culture and those outside the four walls of her play. Aamera played 23 different characters from her life, including neighbors, teachers, aunties and her family. Themes of immigration, islamophobia, near deportation and struggling to fit into a culture that was not the one her parents left behind in India in 1963, emerge throughout Aamera's story. Aamera has performed this play for anti-racism conferences, diversity events, schools, universities, interfaith conferences and more...

One of the favorite comments Aamera received was from a South Asian teen who saw 'American as Curry Pie', and asked, *"Did you have a hidden camera in my house? Because*

*the parents in the play said exactly the same
things as my parents!"*

A review of 'American as Curry Pie':
*https://www.twincities.com/2011/03/20/theater-
review-curry-pie-offers-generous-portions-of-
American-culture.*

Freedom Daze

Ideas like the 'Muslim ban' didn't appear
overnight. Its seeds were planted long before
the 45th President or 9/11. Freedom Daze is a
journey through the media maze of
(mis)information and indoctrination that has
led to the creation of an enemy class of "them."
Using a multi-media approach and weaving
together multiple storylines, the play follows an
artist's quest to discover how a childhood
acquaintance, 'The Girl in the Yellow Dress'
came to be sentenced to a life in solitary
confinement. In a world of 'They hate freedom',
'If you see something, say something' and 'The
Terror Alert is'…where can one find the truth?

Cloth

How much is too much? How little is too little? And who gets to decide?

From the burqa ban in France to dress codes in our own communities, when it comes to women's clothing it seems like everyone has an opinion. CLOTH is a work that explores women's relationship to cloth, covering and choice, and the avalanche of factors influencing that choice.

A review of Cloth: *https://www.talkinbroadway.com/page/regi onal/minn/minn681.html*

Draw Two Circles

A performance art piece that Aamera co-created in 2005, with her theater partner Suzy Messerole, exploring how two women from very different backgrounds, Suzy raised Catholic in a small town in Iowa and Aamera a global citizen raised in Islam, find connection across their differences, through their exploration of patriarchy in society and their religions.

Coming in Fall 2024: *Log Kya Kahenge*

The Khan family is the perfect Desi family with the perfect eldest daughter (let's not talk about the younger one). But beneath the veneer of perfection lies a secret they don't want to confront. 'Log Kya Kahenge' explores mental health stigma, a health care system that isn't culturally responsive and what happens when "What will people say?" becomes the gauge by which you live your life. This play explores themes of societal pressures, mental health and the importance of cultural responsiveness in the mental health system.

Family

For all her work in raising social consciousness, Aamera's primary passion is her family.

She met her husband Kevin, a rock and roll bass guitarist and a music performance venue manager, when he saw her performing on stage in March 2001 at the MN Opera Center. The show was based on Women's history, and was a staged version of 'The House on Mango Street', short stories written by Sandra Cisneros. He was visiting family from his home in Chicago and came backstage to meet her. After reconnecting later that year and a two year courtship, they eloped to Maui and got married in 2003. Her parents, staunch Muslims, initially resistant, accepted Kevin eventually and they had a good relationship till her father passed away in 2006 and her mother in 2023.

Aamera is raising her two daughters, Laila, 16 a budding film director, and Lina, 11 who attends theater camp, in all the philosophies that have shaped her life, and made her the person she is today.

Sealing the relationship in Maui

CHAPTER 7

MADAN'S TRAVEL JOURNAL

Madan is a second generation South Asian, born and brought up in the US. As a very young boy, Madan got to know and love his ancestral homeland from reminiscences and stories recounted by grandparents, parents, aunts and uncles.

On his second visit to India early this year, Madan, a bright and articulate 11 year old, penned a travel journal that gives us 'his' perspective of traveling to and through India.

This narrative is different from the other stories: those poignantly painted the lives of South Asians who had moved to the US, after childhoods spent in South Asia.

Madan was born to first generation parents in Columbus, OH, to an endocrinologist mother and ENT physician father. In many ways he is like any other eleven year old, who loves sports, music and playing with his friends. His favorite subjects are Math and Science and he wants to be an Astrophysicist when he grows up. To that end he studies hard, and does advanced classes in Math and Reading (Greek and Latin Roots).

Naturally, given his career aspirations, his favorite book is 'The Martian', which delved into the science of survival, and escape from Mars. Madan also explores his creative side with music, plays the Cello with his school orchestra and has participated in Piano Recitals with his group. He is good friends with his younger brother Nayan 7, whose ambition is to be a Chef or a Scientist.

The following, in Madan's own words, are his thoughts, feelings and emotions, exploring a country that for immigrant South Asians to the US, was the cradle of our youth.

Madan's Trip to India Journal

Getting There

I've been sitting on a plane for 7 hours. Personally, I don't feel as nauseous as I thought I would be. To fly to India, our trip consisted of three flights, one from Ohio to New York, then to Abu Dhabi, then finally over to India.

Right now, we are heading to Abu Dhabi and the entertainment system and lights shut down, so for most of the time I tried to sleep or just sat in the dark. It was boring, but I had my ipad to play with so I was occupied. Every time I tried to fall asleep, a bright light flashed in my eyes and I woke up with a start as they tried to reboot the entertainment system. It never worked but at least it gave me a fun white light to stare at for twelve hours (just kidding).

Finally we reached India! As I got out of the plane, heat blasted into my face. I was so surprised that I barely felt tired. It was winter in the USA, so we had forgotten about this nice weather. I was thankful I packed shorts. Next, when I got out of the airport I started to notice that people looked a little more like me compared to when I am in the US.

India greeted me with lots of cars honking and lots of people yelling. As we rode in our taxi, I looked around the city. I was astonished that there are so many more cars, and everyone was driving on the left side of the road. What was even more surprising was that the highway signs were in English. I was confused as I thought that people in India speak in Hindi. Then I remembered that the British used to rule India, so everyone probably also learned English around that time.

We pulled into the driveway of Tatamma's house and I noticed that the houses looked very different. They are more square, older, and run down. On the roof, there is another floor which I later learned was a terrace. I entered the door and was greeted by Ammama (grandma) and Tatamma (great grandma). Even though the house looked different, I felt right at home with my family

The Wedding

For the wedding, we went to a resort called Alankrita in Hyderabad. It was a very nice resort with a nice room and lots of nature. The wedding felt really different from an American wedding. There are four sections to an Indian wedding: Haldi, Sangeet, the Wedding, and the Pooja.

The Haldi

The Haldi is the first part of the wedding, where people put yellow powder on the groom and bride's face for good luck. We didn't put the powder on, but we were able to see some family whom I haven't seen for five years. For the Haldi we dressed up in yellow clothes and went over to the ceremony. I was very surprised with the amount of yellow I saw. I was very excited to see all my relatives. A million ammamas came to greet me. Vinny Anna and Anjali Akka (second cousins: bride

Madan and Nayan appropriately dressed in yellow for the Haldi ceremony

and groom) were at the front of the ceremony, but I couldn't see them because of the crowd of people around them.

The Sangeet

The Sangeet is where a bunch of people perform and dance to songs. The music was super loud and we had to scream when we were only a few inches away. This was the same day as the Haldi. The food was amazing and there were lots of meals from different countries. After we ate we sat down to watch the dances. I noticed that for some of the songs, some people didn't know the steps. For one song, no one actually learned the dance but still many of my Tata's (older relatives) went to the front of the stage and danced randomly and looked like they were having the time of their life.

The Ceremony

The wedding was outside, and a lot of things happened there. The baraat started an hour late but I really wasn't surprised because our family is always late. It was cool to see Vinny Anna riding a horse over to the wedding ceremony.

The music was loud, and sometimes I plugged my ears so my ear drums wouldn't blow up. The ceremony place was beautiful with lots of chairs and flowers. I sat down for a bit, but the heat was too intense and I left to stand by a fan.

After a while I started to get hungry, so I went to an indoor area to cool off and get some food. A lot of other people were there too, but I wasn't really surprised. Like I said, it was hot. The food, again, was amazing. I had some trouble finding a seat, because of all the people there.

After that we played some American football with my cousins and that eventually turned into 'Keep Away'. I started to wonder if we were disturbing the rituals at the front of the stage, but then I thought that they were too far away to hear. We made squirt guns with our water bottles and spritzed each other, which really cooled us off. The wedding was like, seven hours in the blazing hot sun. It was fun, but I was relieved it was over too.

I don't know much about the pooja because I wasn't there.

Trip to Charminar

We went to Charminar (a historic monument located in the heart of Hyderabad) or Four Pillars. I sort of thought it would be more clean and nice but that could never be the case with a 400 year old building. It was old and run down with cracks and holes. As we went in line, I could see many people up on the first floor. Charminar really lived up to its name. Char means four, and Minar means pillar. That building literally had four pillars. Personally, I

thought the name was kinda plain but I didn't
have better ideas.

A guy came over and said he was our guide. I
think he had lots of experience being a guide
because he told facts about the building for
what seemed like hours. Then finally he said we
were going up. He led us to a doorway with a
narrow staircase. The staircase was long,
spiraling up to the first floor. The stairs were
huge and I had some trouble getting up, but
after a long time we finally got to the first floor.

I looked around and there were two signs on
the wall. One said "please do not write on
walls" and the other said "please do not spit".
People were not following the first rule for
sure, there were letters sprawled across the
walls saying things like "Joey was here" and "I
like cheese". I wonder why people would do
that. As for the other sign, that didn't even
make sense. Nobody would spit unless
someone put that idea into their head.

The guide led us around the first floor, pointing
out every little thing for us. Every stop he took
one thousand pictures from every angle he
knew. It literally doubled our time there. The
guide told us about secret watch towers to look
at the city. He said people had attacked the
building, so they built a tunnel to another
castle thirty kilometers away. Once he finished
talking, he led us down an even narrower
staircase. At that point I was feeling

claustrophobic. I stumbled once, and sighed with relief when we got down. We walked out of the gates, and I took one last look at Charminar.

Like I said, it wasn't what I expected but it sure was beautiful.

Trip to Goa

The next day we went to Goa, India. It's like a beach town. We went with our cousins.

The house was amazing. It was huge, and there were four floors and a big pool. In the pool we passed the football and played volleyball. My cousins didn't know how to play American football so we taught them the basic rules. We had a football game at the beach and it was fun. Sometimes I got American football mixed up with soccer football. I also jet skied for the first time, which was scary.

The beach was nice, with lots of shells and restaurants at the side. The food and drinks there were really good. They cut a coconut and placed a straw in, which was amazing. It was cool that I was drinking from a real coconut instead of a bottle. The food was very different from American food. Indian food is more spicy and most of the time you eat with your hands. Indian food also involves a lot more rice. I love Indian food so I felt right at home.

Our Trip is Over

I had a lot of fun on our trip. My favorite things were to see my family again, be a part of the wedding, the food, and our trip to Goa. I was sad to leave India but also happy to be back home.

Madan's Key Insights and Takeaways

** Loved visiting India and was disappointed to leave after only two weeks. Could stay for a much longer time.

** It was different from what I expected, especially the houses and bathrooms, but I had a positive experience.

** There was a lot of pollution.

** Enjoyed the hot weather and wearing shorts in winter.

** The food was delicious and spicier. And I liked eating with my hands.

** There were many different animals around, especially the peacocks on the hiking trails.

Under the Banyan Tree

** There are lots of people around you, especially relatives and it was great to play with so many cousins.

** People looked different and "Like Me". I felt right at home.

** Was sad to leave my large extended family, especially my playmates, and would love to go back every few years!

CHAPTER 8

GIVING BACK WHERE NEEDED

Zarina Baber is a Minnesota resident, with 30+ years of experience in causes dear to her heart. This story features her devoted contributions to underserved communities, human rights and politics.

In 2017, AARP Minnesota and Pollen Midwest celebrated Zarina as one of 50 Minnesotans over the age of 50, who live life on their own terms and improve the lives of others at the same time.

Zarina was recognized in the 'Disruptors' category. The link to the Pollen Award story:

https://www.pollenmidwest.org/stories/2017-50-over-50/

Zarina was born in Rajahmundry, Andhra Pradesh, a city on the eastern banks of the Godavari River, to a mother from Chennai and a Surgeon father who served in the Army during World War Two, and after leaving the military joined the Andhra Pradesh Government. Her father's job required moving every 2 years, and Zarina led a nomadic existence till she was 15, when her father retired and settled his family in Hyderabad.

Pioneer Cricketeer

At the age of 17, she broke the glass ceiling in her hometown of Hyderabad, when she became one of the pioneers of the first Women's Cricket team in Andhra Pradesh.

Zarina played 'left handed batsman', and within the short span of a year, helped put the Andhra Pradesh Women's team on the map. They played numerous matches including the Shankerji Memorial Trophy and hosted the New Zealand Women's Cricket Team in 1976. Zarina was also chosen from Andhra Pradesh to play for the South Zone in the Inter Zonal Championships for the Rani Jhansi trophy.

Zarina's pioneering efforts in the early 1970's have continued to reap rewards for Andhra Pradesh and Indian Women's Cricket. In 2017, India's team captain was a woman from Hyderabad, competing globally and second only to England at the 2017 Cricket World Cup.

Early Years

Zarina got married at the young age of 18 and immediately moved to the US to join her husband.

At the time of her nuptials, Zarina was still in her second year of college in Hyderabad, and the move to the US resulted in not finishing her education in India. This did not deter her from pursuing a degree. She enrolled at the University of Iowa, after having to retake her GED's, her studies in India not being recognized.

Zarina went on to complete her BS in Business from the Carlson School of Management,

Zarina with her family at her Bachelor's graduation from University of Minnesota in 1991

University of MN, after her husband's job necessitated a move from Iowa. Later she obtained an MS of Technology Management from the University of St. Thomas, and a Master Certificate from Cornell University in Healthcare Leadership focused on Organizational Change. Zarina is also certified as a Project Management Professional (PMP) and a Certified Scrum Master (CSM).

It's poignant that she got her Undergrad degree the same year as Zameer her older son graduated from elementary school, and obtained her Master's degree the same year as Zameer did!

Career Path

It was inevitable that Zarina's path would lead her to work in the political arena, with 30+ years in Information Technology and Project Management across multiple industries including Healthcare, Retail, Financial Services and 'Government'.

Currently she is the Assistant Commissioner and Chief Transformation Officer in the MN State Office of Transformation and Strategy Delivery, as well as the Chief Business Technology Officer for the Office of Minnesota Governor Walz.

Zarina and Zaheer Baber at the 2020 inauguration of Governor Walz

Volunteerism

In addition to her trailblazing career, Zarina is equally well known for her community and human rights advocacy to underserved populations. She estimated that she would spend 30 to 40 hours a month on volunteer activities, particularly when she founded the Al-Shifa clinic. *"It's not like I'm giving a lot. I feel like I'm getting a lot in return. I need a sense of balance in life and this place provides me and my family with that. I get an opportunity to interact with talented people and I learn so much from that."*

She is a former Board Member of the East Metro Board of the American Cancer Society and Advocates of Human Rights – an international human rights organization representing immigrants and refugees who are victims of human rights abuses, working through education and advocacy to engage the public and policymakers.

Zarina served as spokesperson of a multi-organization coalition advocating for US intervention in Bosnia based on human rights violations. She and her family were also actively involved with the resettlement of Bosnian and Somali refugees in the mid '90s. In addition, she participated in research with Advocates for Human Rights that resulted in a report called "Voices From Silence", that focused on long term impact of post 9/11 on American Muslims.

Zarina has served as the former DFL Anoka County Vice Chair, and is a founding member and current Chair of the national Muslim

Caucus of America, which organized the first National Presidential Candidate Forum in Washington D.C.

Zarina was also asked to speak at the Democratic National Committee (DNC) convention's Muslim Forum.

Al-Shifa Clinic

Zarina was the founder, Volunteer Director and a motivating force behind the Al-Shifa Clinic, providing free health care to Minnesotans of all religions and backgrounds since 1995. Al-Shifa, which means 'to heal' in Arabic, is a volunteer based, part time clinic located at the Islamic Center in Fridley. The clinic serves a clientele of refugee and immigrant populations and all Americans in need.

Physicians in specialties such as Family Practice, Internal Medicine, Pediatrics, Endocrinology, Neurology, Psychology, and Urology were recruited and the clinic partnered with HCMC clinics, North Memorial Medical Center and Allina amongst many other affiliations.
Three other clinics opened in Minnesota based on the Al-Shifa Clinic model, a first of its kind.

"When the concept was brought to me, it fit what I understood growing up in India. My father was a surgeon and he spent his entire

life serving the needy. I grew up with those principles and those values."

"It looks like any typical small medical clinic, but it's totally volunteer based: Every piece of equipment, medication, is donated by the community members, particularly the physicians." Though they had opportunities to seek grants for the clinic, they did not choose that route since it would have, *"taken away from the giving aspect."*

Zarina was chosen a winner in the HCMC 2000 Employee Recognition Program, in the 'Exceptional Recognition to the Community Category for her commitment to the Al-Shifa Clinic.

Future Doctor's Organization

Zarina developed a partnership with Minnesota's Future Doctors organization, (as part of her work with Al-Shifa Clinic), to provide support and create internship opportunities for under-served students. This partnership gave students interested in health care opportunities to network with community physicians and gain valuable experience to enhance their medical school applications. One volunteer was admitted to Mayo Medical School and another as an Emergency Physician in Chicago.

As a result of this initiative, Zarina was a recipient of the Annual Asian Pacific Leadership Award in 2001 and recognized by Senator Mark Dayton in the US Senate the same year. In addition she also received a congratulatory letter from (the late) Senator Paul Wellstone.

Political Candidacy

In 2018, DFL Gubernatorial candidate Rebecca Otto, MN State Auditor, chose Zarina as her running mate for Lieutenant Governor.

Rebecca Otto said at her announcement at the time *"The Minnesota I know and love celebrates the strength that comes from diversity of thought and background. That's why I'm thrilled to welcome Zarina to this ticket, and I'm excited to work with her to build a better Minnesota"*.

Zarina's response was *"The person that drew me into politics and into my lifelong work in health care and human rights was (the late U.S Senator) Paul Wellstone. I see in Rebecca the same compassion and character I saw in Paul."*

Though their ticket lost to Governor Walz and Peggy Flanagan, it vaulted Zarina into the statewide public eye, making her the 'only' person and woman of South Asian origin, and 'only' Muslim woman, to have run for

Statewide office in the United States at the time.

Family Life

Zarina moved to the US in 1976, living first in Chicago, then Iowa and for the past 35 years in Minnesota. She is married to Zaheer Baber who retired from Land O' Lakes as the Regional Director Asia, Middle East, Latin America and Eastern Europe. During his tenure, he worked on projects with the Marines in Iraq as well. They are the proud parents of two sons Zameer and Zafeer.

Zameer, the older son, is the Head of Digital Strategy and Tech Modernization at Point B in Chicago. With a Masters from Oxford University, he is currently pursuing his PHD at IE Business School in Madrid. He is married and has blessed Zarina and her husband with their granddaughter.

Zafeer is an Anesthesiologist and Pain Medicine Physician at Newton-Wellesley Hospital in Boston. He also hosts a show on SiriusXM on Saturdays called 'Medicine in the News'. And, was recently named in Boston Magazine's Top Doctor's issue. He has a little son, giving Zarina and Zaheer another grandchild.

There is no stopping Zarina Baber. She continues to live her life balancing her career and her voluntary activities, and by the lifelong motto that has driven her since her early days!

"I truly believe that if each one of us selected a cause and worked at it, we would be able to help a lot more people."

CHAPTER 9

SOUL CURRY

The power of stories comes when people extend themselves and perform an act of love, service or courage for family, friends and even strangers. They create an image in our minds, touch our hearts and souls and evoke our emotions: laughter, tears and inspiration.

'Soul Curry' features nine short stories from the South Asian community, written in their own voices, that re-create their personal heartwarming experiences.

MEHENDI BY LAKSHMI RAJARAM

'Mehendi laga do didi' ; 'Mujhe Mehendi bahut pasand hai' she expressed excitedly! Padma's voice resonates in my bones even today! She was then, an 8 year old, cheerful, vivacious bubbly personality who just happened to be BLIND!

I wasn't much older, as a 10 year old, it was my first time visiting the School for Blind Girls on behalf of the local Rotary club. The 2 hour scheduled visit lasted upwards of 6 hours as I stood riveted listening to their stories, touched by their souls. Even writing this gives me goosebumps, because after that single momentous day, I returned home profoundly changed!

Sadly the girls at the blind school were orphans, abandoned by their parents for (1) being born a girl child and (2) for being born blind – neither of  which is of their choosing, neither of which they deserved.

Yet, in my frequent visits there, all I received was boundless love, lessons in hope, fueling my passions and aligning my purpose.

The girls recognized me by touch, not just the contours of my body but the essence of my soul. They could sense the difference between Sympathy (towards them), and Empathy, and they always gravitated towards the latter.

I visited the school a dozen times (over the course of 3 years) so they recognized me right away and each time we would spend hours together pursuing their passions, partaking in their desires and being witness to their hopes and dreams.

It was on one such afternoon where they wished me to apply Mehendi/Henna to their palms. I was quite struck by this request...foolishly assuming that they couldn't appreciate the patterns or the bright colors of the wet Mehendi! Was I ever so wrong, as I learned another great lesson that day.

The girls traced the pattern (exactly in their minds) as the coolness of a fine tipped cone of mehendi touched their palms. Their heightened sense of touch gave them acute insight into the designs the wet mehendi created on their hands. And, their keen sense of smell could easily tell the difference between a freshly prepared cone vs. a store bought cone. They were also easily able to sense my energy, and if I was tired after a long day, they would ask me to come back the next day to finish applying Mehendi for the other girls.

Time spent with Padma and others was invaluable and taught me so much. They were every bit bright and beautiful, energetic and talented, and in many ways much more so than others. They understood what they lacked but more than made up for it via their heightened senses and passions (to their advantage). Padma taught me critical life lessons that no school or book would. She and the girls sparked the altruistic gene within me. Time spent in their company left so many indelible imprints, the biggest one being – that just having eyes doesn't mean you can SEE.

SURVIVAL FROM LONG TERM
IMPACT OF BULLYING BY SUMI
MUKHERJEE

This is a story of my battle and survival from a devastating mental illness triggered by bullying. This is based on my first book titled,

Sumi Mukherjee : Author and Speaker

"A LIFE INTERRUPTED: THE STORY OF MY BATTLE WITH BULLYING AND OBSESSIVE-COMPULSIVE DISORDER", which demonstrates a definitive connection between prolonged childhood bullying, Post Traumatic Stress Disorder and the development of one of the more taboo forms of OCD later in life.

Moreover, my most crippling OCD symptoms would consist of mentally picturing images of bullies who had tormented me in the past. These images would soon become further attached with an unspeakable irrational fear... that they would force me to hurt or kill my loved ones if the images were not 'neutralized.'

If you find these concepts difficult to understand at a first glance, you cannot imagine how perplexing they appeared to me as a terrified teen and young man.

The onset of my OCD occurred in May 1992 at the age of 16. For the first five years of my mental illncss, my single greatest struggle and obstacle became simply telling someone what was going on. Instead, I lived a secret life hiding in the shadows being afraid that I was losing my mind. My frightening condition kept me isolated from others and unable to pursue the normal drives of a healthy young man. Friendships were far and few in between, while dating remained out of the question. Before long, merely managing to function through an average day became the greatest challenge of all.

The first success that I can speak about finally came at the age of 21 in 1997, following the loss of my job at a hotel due to my incapacitating symptoms. At last I came out to my family about what was going on, and they were able to get me the therapy and medication that I needed to defeat OCD. But learning about the complex nature of OCD would be a process that would take me several more years to complete. First came a phase of tremendous relief at the realization that I wasn't going crazy after all, and that I would not have to be institutionalized at a psychiatric hospital! Then second, came a major bout of depression and self pity over the fact that I had been diagnosed with this form of OCD. At last, I was able to change my pessimistic perspective, willingly engage in cognitive behavioral therapy and begin to make significant progress with my illness.

During this time period, I was also able to look up and confront my very worst bully from childhood. This most fascinating, revealing encounter helped me to finally deal with the bullying and with the PTSD from my past. Eventually, I was able to derive a lasting positive impact after spending only 16 days in Rogers inpatient treatment facility – a positive impact that has lasted throughout the past several years of my life. I attribute my lasting success to a specific change in my medication regimen made at the facility, as well as their tough approach to ERP (Exposure Ritual Prevention) which I took to heart upon leaving that place. Though my success did not come until several months after I had left Rogers, the change in my meds and the knowledge I had gained would slowly show their purpose over time.

Today, I am thrilled to report that I have finally regained control over my once ever so incapacitating mental illness! Though my ordeal has now reached this much better point, there are millions of other people out there who continue to struggle hard with OCD or other mental illness on a daily basis. I am here to tell those fellow sufferers that this does not have to be their long-term fate. Just as I took back control of my life, they too are capable of freeing themselves from the powerful clutches of this hideous disease or other serious mental health disorders.

ONE SMALL STEP CAN MAKE A HUNDRED DREAMS COME TRUE BY SANTOSH JHANJEE

*Translated from Hindi by Sayali Amarapurkar

My Grandmother is sitting in the courtyard of our house. I am sitting in the lap of my grandmother caressing her gray hair. Every day I used to listen to things she used to hum....

जब लगि तोरी देह है

देह देह कछु देह

देह खेह हो जायेगी

तब कौन कहेगा देह?

Her words meant that as long as you have a body, help the needy.

Under the Banyan Tree

Who will come to seek your help when the body is no more?

Grandma's words started stirring in my mind, when I saw a 10 year old young boy. I saw the desire to learn in his eyes.

It was about 1974 in Delhi when I was working as a teacher in a higher secondary school.

A new water woman was appointed in the school. Her 10-year-old son used to come with her sometimes.

Whenever I used to see him, I saw a unique glow in his eyes, a yearning for learning something that was visible on his face.

My heart told me this kid would do something if he got the chance.

Grandma's talk started resonating in my mind

देह देह कछु देह....

Then what, I took a step forward and got him admitted to our very school where I worked.

My school was co-educational. I took care of his books, education, uniform – and the young lad also did not look back! He made his own and my dreams come true.

Today that young boy is a well known reputed doctor.

My one small step changed the life of a small child, and made his dreams come true!

THANKSGIVING STORY BY
VATSALA MENON

The onset of cold dark evenings and uncertain weather conditions signifies the beginning of a very busy holiday season for most American families. Families far and near make plans to visit relatives, despite soaring airline prices, the hassle of unpredictable weather, and the awkwardness and uneasiness of large family gatherings. Having lived and raised my family here for the last 40 years, I understand the quandary. But large gatherings and unanticipated additions to the thanksgiving dinner do not unnerve my senses. For the first 20 years of my life, large family get-togethers with unexpected guests were considered the norm. Today, while I shop and prep large quantities of food before the imminent Thanksgiving holidays, I have no stress- only joy and excitement to host and provide for the family.

But through the excitement of shopping, planning, and prepping several meals, in addition to organizing sleeping arrangements, an unexplained nagging sensation has begun to settle somewhere deep within my consciousness.

I'm not able to pinpoint the reason for this perplexing feeling of incompleteness. I've tried to be rational and write it off as the dark evenings and the impending long winter. I do what I can for the families in need. Very often, I cook meals for the shelters, and sometimes I just send money to provide meals. But the haunting image and a mild disquiet persists.

Many years ago, during one of my visits to India, I had the opportunity of visiting The Ivor Madom Temple situated in Pampady, a nondescript village, on the southern banks of the Bharathappuzha, the second longest river of Kerala. The temple, enshrined with an aura of holiness, is situated 100 feet above sea level. Massive stone pillars and moss-covered pathways with shelters for many deities surround the main temple premises. The constant rhythm of the river adds to the mystical sensation of the place. People of all walks come there to do rituals for offering peace to the dead.

Under the Banyan Tree

My sisters and I were there for the same
reason. After the early morning rituals for my
only brother, who had an untimely death, we
were all walking down the untrodden and
precarious hillside, content and happy that all
the rituals were performed to our satisfaction.
Close to the temple stood a two-story building
beside a modest church. As we passed by, we
were stopped by a priest. He asked us if we
would like to visit the orphanage and he
pointed to the two-story building. That's when
I looked up and saw, gazing out of the window,
many dark faces of children. Their white toothy
smiles, with skinny long arms, waving
anxiously. Guided by the priest, we went inside
to see the home of orphaned boys. The young
boys from 2 to 14 were eager to show us their
sleeping quarters and art work. The priest
explained that charity kept his kids fed and
clothed. The rooms looked clean but sparse and
well-maintained. When it was time to say

goodbye the little ones clung to us, and to this day, that memory has haunted and followed me around.

We continue to send money whenever we can. My sister in India provides full meals and tells me stories of how happy they are to see her. After so many years, the image of the window in that serene hillside village has never left me. I have given it a lot of thought and have no real answers for these predicaments. Our magnanimity and service does help, but that just clears our guilt and makes us feel good. There is so much more to these troubling questions. I'm sure there are similar homes around the world. I'd like to believe that many goodhearted folks help and provide for them.

But for me the knot in my stomach and the haunting image of the boys from the window, will be a constant reminder that we should be so thankful for what we have, and be willing to share the wealth. I try not to strip off these images from my mind, instead consider it a blessing to be reminded of another kind of life. Every Thanksgiving, and other joyous holidays, I pray that those boys have grown up and crafted a home for themselves, something they never had.

GUARDIAN ANGEL BY ANONYMOUS

It was December 2006, just before Christmas. I went to Charles Schwab to meet our financial advisor, Mark Slocum. Since Christmas was coming up soon, I asked him how his family was planning to celebrate Christmas. Mark said that they probably would not be celebrating Christmas, since his Mother-in-law was sick with cancer. When I heard that, I expressed my sympathies and wished his MIL all the best.

As I was heading back to my car, a thought popped up – *"Why don't you give the 'Guardian Angel' pin to Mark's MIL?"* I always carry a Guardian Angel pin with me in my handbag for sentimental value. I decided to walk back to Mark's office. Luckily he was not busy. I walked over and handed him the Guardian Angel and asked him if he could give it to his MIL.

After that, I completely forgot about the incident and carried on with my life. A month later, I received a card in the mail. I was completely taken aback to see that it was from Mark. This is what he wrote –

> Hello ...
>
> I want to thank you for the guardian angel you gave my mother in law. She was very touched that a stranger to her could be so thoughtful.
>
> Just so you know, she was a strong woman who battled ovarian cancer for 7 years, unfortunately she passed on January 2.
>
> She liked the pin so much that she requested it be placed with her.
>
> My family and myself sincerely appreciate your kindness.
>
> Thank you, Mark Slocum

RETURN OF CONFIDENCE BY RAVIN BHANDARI

It was India's Republic Day Celebration in San Antonio. After the flag hoisting ceremony, we started enjoying the cultural performances by local children and adults. Some of the performances were really good, particularly a song "Aye Mere Watan Ke Logo" sung extremely well by a teenage boy, and the song got a lot of attention from the audience. The cultural program went on.

After 3 or 4 more items another teenage girl entered the stage to present a song. Guess what, she was going to sing the same song too! She appeared very nervous as she thought that her performance would be directly compared with the previous singer. She started singing. Though her singing was fairly good, her expressions showed lack of confidence which were subsiding the total effect of the performance. My wife Amita and I were sitting in the second row and we noticed the problem. We decided that we should send her some encouraging signals. The singing went on. After about two minutes into the song we could make eye contact with the performer. We did not waste even a fraction of a second and gave her a "Thumbs Up" signal. She saw us – she saw our signals. There was a sudden change. Her eyes brightened up with a shiny smile and there was happiness on her face. The performer had got our message that she is performing well and her confidence returned. She completed the rest of the song as if she had sung it the best ever. Song ended with a loud appreciation from the audience.

Usually Thumbs signs are received by the performers from their teachers, parents or known people not from strangers. We did not know the performer nor did she know us.

Encouraging a talent to regain her confidence was a very rewarding experience to both of us.

In our everyday life people get many occasions to pass on emotions of love, hope, faith, encouragement, morale boosting etc to others. One must really grab such opportunities to pass on some good feelings to make someone's day special.

In Picture: Ravin with Amita at Republic Day 2023 celebration in San Antonio

---

KINDNESS OF STRANGERS BY PREETI MATHUR

When my brother and I were little, we would accompany our parents on occasional Sunday evenings to visit their friends' homes. While they chatted and visited, we would keep ourselves amused with made-up games. In one of those homes, *the uncle,* an executive with Air India, had a large glass "showcase," – an etagere filled with souvenirs from his travels worldwide. I remember sitting glued to it, fascinated, with the two of us trying to outguess each other on the origins of each memento.

I like to think that is perhaps where my passion for travel began. That, and the bedtime stories my father would tell us. Often, he would read the adventures of Sinbad the Sailor or Hatim al-Tai from books in his library. Many nights he would also make up stories from his imagination—about a gamekeeper's family who lived in a treehouse in Salisbury, South Africa, and whose children went on adventures around the world with pixies and fairies.

After getting married, I found that my husband, Anoop, fortunately shared my love of travel. As a family and later by ourselves, we have traveled extensively in our 44 years together. He is an ace planner, meticulously researching things to see and do, and the most efficient and cost-effective ways to travel. We also share similar ideas regarding travel outcomes, places to visit, and where to stay. Rather than check off a list of things to see and do, we both love to spend time interacting with locals, which is why we always prefer staying in B&Bs or smaller hotels rather than large, high-end chains.

Travel has opened many doors for us and taught us in ways no textbook can. It has helped us connect with people and cultures vastly different from ours. Yet, with each trip, we have come back, realizing that despite all the differences, we are all the same—human beings with similar wants and needs and the same capacity to give to others, even if they are strangers.

The kindness of strangers on our trips, even when things were not going well, has reinforced our faith in humanity. It has made us intrepid travelers—ready to explore and try anything (within reason, of course!). I could share several stories and experiences of how fellow travelers or locals helped us, but this one of how a stranger went out of his way to help us tops them all. This trip was back in the early 1990s, before we had the Internet, GPS, or mobile phones. I had joined Anoop in Brussels at the end of a work-related course he was attending. After exploring the city, we rented a car to drive to the medieval town of Brugges via Waterloo. As we left the car rental place, we found ourselves stuck on the Centrum—the city's center. Round and round we went looking for the exit that would take us out of Brussels. Finally, in exasperation, Anoop took the nearest way out, and we found ourselves on a narrow street in front of a cafe. Since I know a little French, I hopped out to ask for directions. A man eating his breakfast began giving them to me in rapid French, which was way beyond what I had learned in college. Finally, when he realized he was not getting through, or perhaps seeing the desperation on my face, he left his breakfast and came out. He gestured to me to hop at the back and then seated himself in the passenger seat. Following his hand gestures, we drove more than a mile out before he made us stop and pointed to the correct exit. He then hopped out of the car, waving away our money offer. Repeatedly saying Bon Voyage, he turned and walked away. We were unsure how he made it back to his breakfast which must have become stone cold.

But his kindness, sans any expectations towards people he would never meet again, left much warmth in our hearts that we still remember today.

मैं और मेरी आजादी की चादर! BY
SANTOSH JHANJEE

आज नई पीढ़ी जिस आजादी की चादर ओढ़ कर चैन और शांति की नींद सो रही है, जब कभी उसकी तहे एक-एक कर खुलने लगती है, तब अनायास ही मेरे चेहरे पर मुस्कान, गर्व और आंखों में आंसू और उदासी छा जाती है.

इस चादर की एक एक परत में आंसू भी है और मुस्कुराहट भी.

बात १९४६ -४७ की है. मैं १०-१२ साल की थी. देश में "अंग्रेजों भारत छोड़ो" का आंदोलन जोरों पर था. गली-गली नारे लगाते, जोश से भरे भारतीय जुलूस निकालते. सुबह सवेरे देशभक्ति के गीत गाते, प्रभात फेरी निकलती. जोशीले नौजवानों पर लाठियां बरसती, गोलियां चलती, फांसी को दुल्हन मान उस पर देश भक्त हंसते-हंसते लटक जाते!

देशभक्ति के इस जोश को देखकर हम बच्चों के मन में भी देश प्रेम हिलोरे मारने लगा. पड़ोस के और घर के सब बच्चों ने मिलकर तय किया कि हम भी जुलूस निकालेंगे. हम सब ने मिलकर पेपर से छोटे-छोटे झंडे बनाए और उन्हें लेकर गली में नारे लगाते हुए दोपहर में जब सब सो जाते हैं हम निकल पड़ते. हमारे नारे कुछ इस तरह होते थे: मेरा भाई इस टोली का लीडर था,

भाई नारा लगाता : नौजवानों!

हम कहते: हां जी !

भाई नारा लगाता: काम करोगे?

हम कहते: क्या जी?

भाई नारा लगाता: जेल चलोगे?

बच्चे कहते: हां जी.

भाई नारा लगाता: चीज मिलेगी!

बच्चे कहते: क्या जी?

भाई नारा लगाता: आजादी

हम सब बच्चे कहते: आजादी.. आजादी.. आजादी..
कहकर जोर-जोर से हंसते!

हमारा शोरगुल सुनकर बड़े-बड़े मूछों वाले अंग्रेज गार्ड आ
जाते. उनके हाथों में लंबी बंदूक और पैरों में लंबे जूते होते,
जिन्हें देखकर हम ना दाएं देखते ना बाए, और जो घर
सामने दिखाई देता, डरकर उसी में छिप जाते. हमारा रोज
का यह काम था. उन दिनों की इस घटना को याद कर
आज भी होठों पर हंसी और आंखों में आंसू आ जाते हैं.

उन दिनों कर्फ्यू लगता था. बाहर निकलना मना था और
उस समय घरों में फ्रिज तो होते नहीं थे. कर्फ्यू लगने
वाला है तो महीने भर का सामान लाकर रखते. मेरी बहन

बहुत छोटी, लगभग १ साल की थी और रात को दूध के लिए रोने लगी. घर में दूध नहीं था. मेरी मां ने उसे चुप कराने की बहुत कोशिश की पर वो रोती ही रही. फिर माँ ने आटा पानी में घोलकर और छानकर बोतल में भर कर उसे दिया. वह रोते-रोते इतना थक चुकी थी कि उसे ही पीकर सो गई. इस आजादी की चादर में हम बच्चों की खिलखिलाहट है और आंसू भी! इसे संभाल कर

रखिएगा और याद भी करते रहिएगा !

Photo Courtesy: Kids Britannica
https://kids.britannica.com/students/article/Quit-India-campaign/313113

Determination Cuts The Shackles Of Dilemma By Santosh Jhanjee

---

*Translated from Hindi by Sayali Amarapurkar

Sometimes an incident happens in our life that changes the direction /course of our life. Something said by someone makes such a deep impact on us that we make the impossible possible. One such incident changed the course of my life.

I was probably twelve years old then, used to study in 6th grade.

Till then I used to speak in a lisp. People used to understand my words only partially/half-heartedly.

Even in appearance I was the least beautiful in the family. That's why feelings of inferiority had settled deep in my mind.

I was shy to meet people, or to talk to them.

I used to hide if someone came to the house.

Once my maternal uncle came home and sat for four hours and hiding from him I sat under the cot for four hours!

But the incident I want to tell you happened right after this :

My elder sister was very dominant in the family and we were all afraid of her. That day she was scolding me on some issue and I kept on replying back to her, and arguing with her. That's when my sister's friend, whose name was Pushpa, came there. Seeing me answering and arguing with my elder sister, she said, "Don't you have any shame, you are talking back to your elder sister? First become something, become like them, then think of arguing with them".

Just then, "First become something..," that single sentence changed my life! This sentence haunted me day and night. It wreaked havoc in my mind. I made up my mind that now I have to become something. I practiced speaking in front of the mirror for hours every day. And slowly my lisp started reducing and I started speaking properly. I told myself everyday that "I can do something!"

I put my soul into studying and moving forward.

And today when I speak, people say that they forget to even blink.

Don't take someone's words negatively, take them positively, and your life will change.

Santosh as a young girl

CHAPTER 10

A LIFETIME OF 'SEVA'

Kumud Kamran is a woman of true 'Seva' or service to her immediate and extended circle of family, friends and community.

Her home was affectionately coined Grand Central Station by her children, as the doorbell was always ringing, someone was 'stopping by' to drop something off, pick something up or just to say Hello! Kumud greeted all callers with a smile, ready to serve tea and a snack. Her home was the first stop for many families moving to the US and Minnesota, as they transitioned to their own lives or were stopping by for medical, job or other reasons. As her daughter Poornima says *"we often did not sleep in our own beds, as we were ready to welcome a new family to stay with us"*.

All this, while running a household of six, sometimes ten, working full time as an Engineer and raising two busy children!

Early Life

Kumud was born in Hyderabad, India and raised by her maternal grandparents after her father passed away when she was 6 years old. She grew up in an extremely erudite household, her mother teaching Hindi and Sanskrit at the Nanak Ram Bhagwandas College, and her grandfather exerting broad influence as the Secretary of Finance, Planning and Education in the Government. Arts and Culture were a deep influence in her younger years as her grandfather promoted amateur artists, singing and dancing and had a street inaugurated in his name: LN Gupta Lane.

Kumud married Kunal Kamran at the age of 19, and joined him in Minnesota soon after. Though she was pursuing a Core Sciences degree in Botany, she was unable to complete her exams with the move to join her husband. Kunal had been here since 1966, to pursue graduate studies at the University of Minnesota, and was a Mechanical Engineer who founded his own company in the 1980's.

As with most new brides coming from a large combined family, the first year was difficult and lonely, alleviated to some degree, when she started her Undergrad degree course at the University of Minnesota. She temporarily put that on hold when her in-laws came to live with them in Minnesota, and welcomed their son Sujan in 1972 and daughter Poornima in 1976.

Geeta Ashram Movement

One of the proudest pursuits for Kumud and her husband Kunal, with strong encouragement from their in-laws, was their service to the Geeta Ashram movement. Founded by Indian Independence activist Swami Hariharji Maharaj, the movement is rooted in ancient tradition and the Bhagvad Geeta holy text, and encourages a spiritual approach to all aspects of life. In Minnesota, the Geeta Ashram was registered in 1975, with the group meeting at the homes of different members. The membership grew from a dozen families to more than 600, and in 1987 the Kamran's played a significant role in helping to establish a major Center, to house its offerings and services in Brooklyn Park.

The Geeta was at the core of the family's foundation. The 12th chapter was recited every evening before dinner, and conversations and birthday blessings centered on the core values of the Geeta. After the Ashram was built, the family attended weekly 'Satsangs'.

As Kumud's daughter says *"I realize now how much my parents sacrificed. There were no social events, football games or even school events which would stand in the way of the weekly 'Satsangs'. We learned service: bringing homemade food in large pots to feed 50-100 people, preparing the mandir, serving prasad, and cleaning up. We would spend 3-4 hours there each Sunday.*

I continue to see my mother's commitment to the Ashram and the Ashram 'family'- only

missing events when her mother needs her or the weather does not allow her to drive there".

Receiving Service Award from Geetha Ashram

Career and Volunteerism

"My mother was always moving! There are very few memories of her actually sitting down and chatting while we were at home" says her son Sujan.

Staying home, bringing up her kids, caring for her in-laws, Kumud still managed to continue her education, and obtained her Bachelors of Science in Chemistry and Biological Sciences from the University of Minnesota. Over the subsequent years, she obtained many other certifications that included Green Belt, Mini MBA and Internal Auditor.

She trail-blazed a path for herself as a hands-on Chemical engineer in the early days of the computer 'printed-circuit board' manufacturing. She demonstrated that determination and hard work were foundational to progress, and had a stellar career as a Senior Quality Engineer in Product Development, R&D and Design Assurance for companies that ranged from: Honeywell; to Boston Scientific; to St. Jude Medica; to Urology, Inc; to American Medical Systems. Her successful career spanned nearly 30 years, all the while juggling family and a myriad of other obligations.

Kumud finally retired in 2019 at the age of 68, at the insistence of her children. They wanted her to enjoy life! But Kumud could not sit still and dived wholeheartedly into volunteerism, conducting experiments for kids at the Science Museum, tutoring English through the Literary Council to Somali, Thai and Laotian immigrants. This was a continuation of the early volunteering she did when she first arrived in the 1970's.

Family

Kumud held her kids to the same high standards she had set for her own career, whether it was academics, extracurricular activities or community service. This set the foundation for their role as parents today.

She was the driving force for Sujan to join the Boy Scouts. She foresaw the values alignment between her own principles and scouting, along with social and leadership benefits. She was uncompromising about his attendance at Monday evening Scout meetings.

Similarly, she enabled Poornima to excel at Bharatnatyam classical dance and music.

Sujan lives in San Francisco with his wife and children. After a long and successful career at Intel as an electrical engineer, he now works in Strategic Planning for a start-up company in the 'Cloud' chip business. Sujan says *"The impact of mom's compassion, determination and commitment is indelible. She instilled a foundation of self-reliance and commitment to excellence, which guides me across all facets of life"*.

Poornima is a respected Pediatrician with a medical degree from Boston University and lives in the Twin Cities area with her husband and two children. *"I continue to flash back to my childhood and find my 'motherly instincts' replicating her thoughtfulness"*.

Kumud's 5 Grandchildren

An Ongoing Chapter
Kumud has had the exemplary ability to simultaneously excel as a wife, parent, professional and community leader. Her son Sujan says *"she demonstrates a level of discipline and*

organization with such graceful efficiency that she was un-phased to talk on the phone, cook four things on the stove and help us with our homework simultaneously. We learned that it may not be possible to do "everything", but with the right planning and focus, it is possible to accomplish far more than we could otherwise imagine".

Today, her children *"beg"* her to put herself first, take better care of herself, and allow them to help her, to little avail. She continues to follow her lifelong principles of 'love Seva', putting others needs ahead of her own and is devoted to the care of her 93 year old mother who lives with her, always with a smile on her face.

Kumud dancing Kathak as a young bride at Diwali

And, the young Kathak dancer who twirled away as a girl, and performed her last dance as a young bride, at the Diwali celebration of the India Association of Minnesota in 1970, eyes filled with dreams, fulfilled those abundantly, with the greatest humility, in a lifetime of service and give back.

CHAPTER 11

THIS GRANDMA IS UNBELIEVABLE

S arla Arora is a grandma extraordinaire and dynamic 83 year old.

Sarla was born in 1939 in Multan, Pakistan. She came from a large family of 8, 5 sisters and 3 brothers. After Independence, the family left everything behind and moved to the Punjab, close to Delhi. Her father was a cloth merchant and away from home for long periods of time plying his trade. Daily life was very difficult and resources were few and far between. Sarla recalls the days of her youth, walking to the nearest pond balancing baskets of laundry on her head, and carrying pails of water back for the family's daily use. Even 'one anna' was hard to come by for milk and vegetables and they subsisted often on plain flour and water.

Sarla's father was a freedom fighter and very involved in the 'Quit India' movement launched by Mahatma Gandhi. He instilled in Sarla life long values of service, enterprise and national pride. Being a cloth merchant, he objected to the British export of Indian cotton and was vocal in the 'Wear Khadi' movement.

Her parents also strongly believed in learning, and supported Sarla in her quest for higher education. She endured physical hardship getting to school and later studying for her 'Teacher's' qualifications. Of note is the fact that she taught for over 40 years, and her students benefited from her tutoring in multiple subjects including History, Geography, Civics, and the Arts: Painting, Cooking, Sewing and Singing. Her days were long and Sarla's mode of transportation was a bicycle, and later the train to Delhi, first for her training and subsequently her job.

Sarla got married in 1968 and moved to Delhi where she not only obtained a Masters but continued to influence the lives of new generations of students by indulging her love of teaching.

The couple were blessed with their only son Sundeep in 1971, and a beautiful and loving daughter when Sundeep married his wife Rakhi in 1997. Sarla's first trip to her future home in the US was on the auspicious occasion of the births of her twin grandsons Ram and Krishan in 2006.

Sarla's devotion and deep love for her family is evident in the songs she has written and performed.

Sarla moved permanently to the US in 2015, after her husband passed away. Her son is a successful Pediatric doctor in the Twin Cities area. She reinvented herself by immersing in different activities and establishing deep friendships.

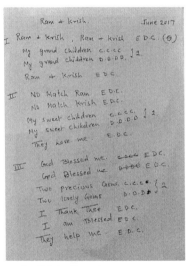

An Ode to Grandsons

Having never played the piano in her life, she started taking piano lessons with her grandsons, composing and singing religious and patriotic songs and also having fun with popular Bollywood music.

The Performer

She took piano lessons with Galina Belssar resulting in bi-annual recitals. Sarla performs before a packed and enthusiastic audience, both solo pieces and duets with her grandsons.

Galina Belssar waxes poetic about Sarla.

"She is amazing. She started playing piano at the age of 76, previously having only played the harmonica which is completely different. Learning from scratch, practices diligently and sets a fantastic example for my students. Overcoming two knee replacements she continues to bloom like the best flowers in the world. She composes her own songs and we sing together. She has taught me a lot about Indian culture and religion. I wish I had more students like her. I cannot live without her delicious Indian Parathas. This Grandma is unbelievable!"

Daily Life

Sarla gets up early in the morning and after an hour long Pooja, she spends her time doing yoga, gardening, cooking, sewing, playing piano and composing and singing 'Bhajans'.

Her 'pooja' alcove pays homage to 'Saraswati', Durga Ma', 'Mahakali', 'Radha-Krishna', 'Ganesh', 'Shiva', 'Ram and family' and 'Lakshmi' among many other deities.

Prayer Area For Pooja

Her vegetable and herb garden flourish under her green thumb and being a fantastic cook she grows the essentials which are utilized in her daily creations. Her gardening skills are also showcased in her beautiful flowers.

Citizenship

Eight years after permanent residency in the US, Sarla proudly became a US citizen. Not only did she study hard for the interview, she aced her exam and was complimented profusely by her interviewer for her knowledge and confidence.

Good Friendships

Sarla has established a wide group of friends. They have joined Sarla in celebrating birthdays and special occasions and she is very active in the Hum Senior group, an event organized by the non-profit organization AshaUSA.

Sarla loves to entertain and concocts delicious meals for her family and friends. Her dishes at the 'Hum Group potluck get togethers' are eagerly consumed.

Family

Being surrounded by her family is a critical component of Sarla's life. She displays her love for her family by composing endless poems in their honor.

And, for Sarla, in the final count, it all comes down to being the best mother to her small clan.

CHAPTER 12

CURIOUS! COLLABORATIVE! HIGHLY MOTIVATED!

T he talented and versatile Akhil Kollengode, is an 18 year old at the University of Minnesota, Rochester (UMR).

Looking Ahead

As the University of Minnesota (UMR) prepared to welcome its first batch of students in the Fall of 2022, to its: ***NXT GEN MED:*** (*https://r.umn.edu/academics-research/undergraduate-programs/bshs/nxt-gen-med*), a new accelerated Health Sciences program in collaboration with the Mayo Clinic and Google Cloud, Akhil Kollengode was one of 10 freshmen enrolled in the program.

A program that will wrap up his Bachelor of Science degree in 2 and a 1/2 years instead of 4 years!

Growing up, Akhil's futuristic mindset continually drove him to think about 'What's Next'. His mother was keen on a Technology and IT future, but Akhil was interested in

Medicine. His goal was to be a Cardio Thoracic surgeon, but the prospect of 8+ years of Medical school was daunting, and he did not know if he had the determination and strive for that length of time. He wanted to apply himself to the workforce as soon as possible.

There was pressure from friends and family: *"In Indian culture everybody has an opinion. All Asians want to be a doctor. But, your life is your life! It's your responsibility! It's your choice! You have to take initiative and take action"*. So, he chose an unconventional and trail blazing program that will allow him to contribute to the world of medicine in a unique and different way: in the high demand fields of digital health, data and analytics, human-centered design and project management.

His peers, Akhil says, are often 'amazed' when he tells them about the unorthodox college path he is taking. His motivation is to go *'straight into the work field within the shortest amount of time possible'*. Like many High School graduates, Akhil was tempted to leave Rochester, MN where he grew up, and explore a higher educational climate away from home. But in the end, he opted to attend the University in his hometown, for the prospect of graduating early (saving a semester's worth of costs from his college price tag: about $15,000), a paid internship at the Mayo Clinic and opportunities for significant scholarship dollars.

Participating in NXT GEN MED's 'Summer Quest' program, while still in High School, he toured and stayed at the University (UMR) campus in downtown Rochester, met professors, and heard from experts at the Mayo Clinic. *"It was super interactive and hands-on, which I am a big fan of. It also opened my eyes to some fields in healthcare that are not patient facing and yet highly rewarding"* (ranging from figuring out how to deploy a vaccine in a global pandemic to looking at how patients interact with physicians through telemedicine).

Thus, if all goes according to plan, Akhil will be handed his college degree in December 2024, while his peers following the traditional college path will still be working hard, a year and a half away from graduation.

Family Life

Akhil was born in Chalakudy, Kerala and adopted soon after his birth, by his parents Anantha (Andy) Kollengode and Ganga Gopalkrishnan. The family which includes his younger sister Anushka, also adopted as a baby from the same facility in Chalakudy, moved to Rochester, MN when he was two years old, because his parents had jobs at the Mayo Clinic: His father is an Operations Manager, Radiation Oncology and is the Assistant Professor of Health Care Systems Engineering, and his mother is an Information Security

Manager and Unit Head – IT. His younger sister Anushka is a RISE scholar (RISE Up and RISE High programs that connect underrepresented kids with potential, to successful mentors) and has used a $500 scholarship from the Ann Bancroft Foundation to develop an App to reduce litter.

The family traveled widely when Akhil was growing up, exposing the children to new

cultures and experiences, and grounded Akhil and Anushka in their heritage with frequent visits home to Kerala and Tamil Nadu in India.

Akhil and his sister had an idyllic and busy childhood growing up. The family was highly cultured with Akhil's father playing the Mridangam (a percussion instrument also known as a tabla), and his mother performing and teaching Mohiniyattam (originated in Kerala) and Bharatanatyam (originated in Tamil Nadu) Indian Classical dance. Akhil specialized in Carnatic music but is not able to perform as much as he would like, due to his focus on college and the time constraints that come with it.

The family celebrated all the festivals with gusto, with Diwali being a favorite. Akhil and his sister enjoyed the preparations that went into celebrating Diwali, such as making the colorful sand paintings called Rangoli.

In 2018, for the first time, the Minnesota Children's Museum of Rochester celebrated Diwali. Akhil's mother Ganga is quoted as saying *"It's a joy to share our culture and also our celebration with the newer generations here in Rochester"*. Ganga is a member of the Rochester Vidhyalaya, a

nonprofit organization promoting music, arts, culture and education. Akhil, a 14 year old at the time, performed the song 'Azhage Azhage' in Tamil, which is about 'noticing the beauty of nature like in the rain or in a peacock'.

The All-Rounder

Akhil was on the Mayo School Boys Swim and Dive team since 2014, and was swimming since he was 5 years old. In explaining his commitment to the team

"I choose to continue with the Mayo Boys Swim and Dive team because it is such a fun sport and the boys are like a second family."

Given his aptitude for music, Akhil sang the National Anthem at every Swim and Dive Team Home Meet.

He also was a part of school-based singing groups and was with the Honors Choir group for many years

Akhil was a finalist for the 2017 Next Generation Storytellers contest, presented by Bolder Options Rochester and The Med City Beat. The subject matter of his story, related to his interest in music, was his Honor Choir director. His respect for Mr. Johnson stemmed from many reasons, particularly Mr. Johnson's advice on 'the recipe to a happy and good life is to find your talent and use it to help other people'. This advice has stayed with Akhil since 7th grade, and he uses it as a beacon every day.

In 2023, Akhil was one of 10 South Asians of all ages, who was chosen to represent his age group in recording a video to promote civic engagement: encouraging youth that had just turned of voting age to vote. The video was sponsored through ICAM (Indian Cultural Association of Minnesota: icamn.org) in partnership with United Ways and Minnesota Council of Nonprofits (MCN). The video can be seen at the YouTube link: *https://www.youtube.com/watch?v=NO_f-UvWO1k*

A Bright Future

Akhil has been described as *"a compassionate youth, interested in art, community services, a competitive swimmer and a musician specializing in Carnatic Music"*. He is multilingual, speaking both Malayalam and Tamil reflecting the origin of his parents hailing from Kerala (mother) and Tamil Nadu (father). He was a first time voter, and did his bit to encourage others of his generation to vote. He has embarked on his freshman year at University of Minnesota, Rochester (UMR), determined to get his Health Science degree in 21/2 years and join the workforce as soon as possible. At just 18, the world is his oyster, and he is determined to fulfill his dream of living in Colorado or wherever life takes him.

Family Vacations to India are still highly anticipated and enjoyed. It enables Akhil to connect with his roots and re-establish where he came from.

As he so poignantly puts it, it allows him to *"relive life but starting from Day One"*

CHAPTER 13

GOOD WILL AMBASSADOR

P rakash Puram's moniker 'Prakash', metaphorically designates the bearer as a source of 'enlightenment or wisdom'. For his family and friends, Prakash has made this world a better place, through the illumination, guidance and help he has selflessly provided all his life.

PRAKASH PURAM
Minneapolis, Minnesota

Cool dude, great dad, love to help people even if it means I have to kill myself to do that. I am a risk taker and willing to abandon all success and pursue a quest for greater expansion of my knowledge.

In celebration of his 60th birthday, an 85 page photo book titled 'Words from the heart', was lovingly created by his close family and friends. Over a hundred stories capturing the 'essence' of Prakash – – from his childhood, to his academic achievements in India and the US; stellar career path from 'Unilever' to 'Pillsbury' to 'IBM' to 'Honeywell' to 'Net Perceptions' to CEO of 'iXmatch'; public policy and political appointments ranging from 'President Bush's Export Council' to the 'Federal Reserve Bank

Advisory Council', and the Board of the 'University of Minnesota Medical Foundation' – – filled the closely packed pages and are bulleted below.

*Humorous *Resilient *Lung power *Big heart *High achiever *Helpful *Smart *Brilliant memory *Long lasting friendships *Mentor *Master Networker *Flaming Extrovert *Private Pilot's license holder *Well Spoken *Empathetic *Ambitious *Multi-lingual (6 languages including Russian, Japanese) *Personable *Knowledgeable *Hospitable: Home affectionately known as 'Puram Motel' *Relentless *Implacable *Perseverance and tenacity in the face of adversity * Magnanimous *Never-say-die attitude *Focused *Guiding light *24X7 *Envied Rolodex *Kamala the secret sauce to Prakash's success- – long leash that allows Prakash to juggle a thousand balls at one time!

Early Years/Philanthropy

Prakash was born and raised in Madras, India. From his early years, he exhibited the traits enumerated above, and which were to become his hallmark.

In school, looking for nothing more than a volunteer experience to list on his resume, he offered to escort a catholic nun around his hometown of Madras, India. He got more than he bargained for. The nun was none other than 'Mother Teresa'. Prakash, a student at a Jesuit college did not even recognize her name. *"I had gone to the school principal and told him I was worried about finding a job after graduating, and he said I should expand my resume by doing community service"*

For the next year, Prakash accompanied Mother Teresa on visits to government leper homes. Watching her tender ministry to India's outcasts, left a profound impression on him. In his final year at college, he led a student run campaign to raise money for Mother Teresa's work with lepers.

Throughout his impressive corporate career at Pillsbury, Honeywell and IBM, he made time to volunteer with poor and disabled people. *"All of the stuff I do in my spare time, the community service portion of it, has been a direct result of the encounter and impression Mother Teresa made on me 40+ years ago. I have never been able to get her out of my mind. She's like a hologram".*

With Mother Teresa prodding his conscience, Prakash volunteered at Courage center in the Twin Cities, an organization that provides service to 20,000 disabled people,. He took clients shopping, to the movies, made tie-dyed T-shirts and played basketball with them. He became a Board member and was named Chairman of the Public Policy committee, lobbying on behalf of disabled people in the Minnesota state legislature. He also sent money to leper homes in India, volunteered with Meals on Wheels, the Special Olympics and Storefront/Youth action, an agency that provided counseling programs and violence prevention for suburban youth.

A Life Partnership

Prakash and Kamala got married in June 1979, while he was a management trainee at Unilever in India. Soon after, he moved to the US to pursue an MBA at the University of Minnesota. Kamala, still finishing her MBA, joined him in 1980. Though initially hesitant about the move, Prakash convinced Kamala to come to Minnesota, by assuring a move back, if 'she did not like living in the US'. 42 years later they have spawned a productive and happy marital partnership, two successful sons and daughters-in-law and 4 granddaughters and one grandson.

Kamala is a successful and driven individual in her own right. In a crazy four month period in 1983, she obtained an MBA in Management Information Systems, gave birth to her oldest son, signed house papers from her hospital bed and moved into their new home with an infant, and started a job at Cenex.

She held senior level management positions at Fortune 500 companies, co-founded her own company iXmatch (next generation real life technology matching people's skills to job requirements), and was a management consultant for four years. After being diagnosed with breast cancer in 2009, she plunged into the non-profit world to create a more meaningful life. She worked at Sewa-AIFW as an Executive Director and then started her own non-profit, 'Asha USA' with a Bush Fellowship Grant.

Academics

Prakash has an impressive academic and professional resume. He obtained a Bachelor of Science from Loyola College in Chennai, a Business Management Diploma from Xavier Labour Relations Institute, Jamshedpur, an MBA from the University of Minnesota and a Master of Public Administration from Harvard University.

Ukraine Market Reform

After receiving his third post graduate degree from Harvard's John F Kennedy School of Government in 1993, and on academic leave from IBM, he embarked on a three month summer project in the Ukraine, touring all the major cities using Kiev as a base. The project sought to institute economic reform in the Ukraine. His Harvard thesis, focused on joint ventures, privatization and retail wholesale distribution networks, served him well on the Ukrainian project. He worked with the Ministry of Economic Reform headed by the ex-Prime Minister, to introduce free market systems to a country that had only known state owned enterprise systems.

Prakash traveled to over a 100 countries for business and pleasure and also attended the World Economic Forum in Davos for three years as a Harvard Designate.

Public Policy

Besides his corporate career successes, Prakash was actively involved in Public Policy and Republican politics. He was appointed by President Bush to be a member of the President's Export council and also the Federal Reserve Bank of Minneapolis Advisory Council on Small Business and labor. He also supported John McCain in his Presidential bid.

He used his extensive networking contacts to do good and help others: have the US Army airlift a CT Scan machine urgently needed in Tamil Nadu, India and facilitate much needed student and work visas.

Advising John McCain's Presidential Bid

Olympic Torch Bearer

If Prakash had selected the centennial Olympic torchbearers himself, they would be as noble and accomplished as Martin Luther King Jr. or Mahatma Gandhi. Instead, after a nomination by his young sons, he was chosen by the United Way (in recognition for a lifetime of volunteerism and embracing the Olympic spirit), to be one of 34 local community heroes to carry the flame for a 2/3 mile distance through the Twin Cities, before it went on its way to the Atlanta Olympics in 1996.

He practiced for his leg of the Olympic relay by jogging with a 4 pound weight taped to a broom. *"There is a lot of pressure. The torch gets heavy and you don't want to drop the sucker. It's overwhelming. I am not a runner or an athlete and being chosen is proof that parents can be role and community models. The important message is that community service is very important".*

Parkinson's Diagnosis

In 2002 Prakash and his family were devastated to receive his diagnosis of Parkinson's disease. He was told that he had a decade before his condition would incapacitate him. Eager to fully exploit the good times that he had left, Prakash swam, gardened, and performed his duties as CEO of iXmatch as he always had, but with a little more 'gusto'. Most notable, it was after his diagnosis that he was elected to the President's Export Council from 2004-2008 and the Federal Reserve Bank Advisory Council from 2008-2010.

But as the years went by, his prescribed medications lost their effectiveness and his symptoms, once merely inconvenient, soon became debilitating. His 'on' time shrank from 95 percent to 20 percent of his day. His family and friends watched helplessly as his vivacious personality faded with debilitating tremors and freezing. Prakash and Kamala sold their company iXmatch in 2010, and Prakash withdrew from all active life. Kamala, despite being diagnosed with breast cancer and undergoing chemotherapy, became his full time caregiver.

Fed up with his situation, and motivated by his son Sidharth's upcoming wedding in India, at which he was determined to be a participant in the festivities and not a passive attendee, Prakash hunted for other options. Through his Parkinson's support group, he learned about Medtronic DBS Therapy, a treatment that used a surgically implanted device to deliver carefully controlled electrical stimulation to targeted areas of his brain. Though there were side effects, and he had to have his settings optimized twice, the therapy helped Prakash reclaim the active life he thought he had lost.

Within a couple of weeks of his surgery, Prakash and Kamala (now cancer free), made several trips across the US to visit family and friends, and within three months attended Sidharth's wedding in India. Prakash participated in all the activities: dancing, socializing, organizing and coordinating all the details associated with the wedding, including performing multiple cartwheels, surprising the audience so soon after his brain surgery.

Always eager to give back and share his bounty, Prakash became part of the Medtronic Ambassador Program and was on the University of Minnesota Medical Foundation and Neuroscience Development Advisory Committee. He became a trusted source for several Parkinson's patients considering the surgery. Many of the Medtronic referrals were minorities and/or of American Asian heritage. He also helped with fundraising, by identifying high end benefactors and matching them with research opportunities at the University of Minnesota.

As a friend aptly said, *"if a cure for Parkinson's is to be found, it will not be because of celebrities like Michael J Fox but because Prakash got involved"*.

Goodwill Ambassador

One of Prakash's most celebrated traits is 'Master Networker'. What is endearing about it, is how he has used it to forge life long friendships from chance encounters.

Pope Blessing In Rome

Notable among these, is the story of a young Japanese woman (Masako Yamamoto), he met in line at 'Sbarro's Pizza' and invited her to stay at his home. The next time the family visited Japan, a limousine was sent by her father, Teruhiko Yamamoto (a prominent Industrialist and chairman of Tak Companies, a subsidiary of Fujitsu) to pick them up at the airport. They were treated to a royal tour of Kobe City, Japan with access to shrines and places not open to public access.

Another delightful story is his encounter with a Finnish couple, Risto and Christina at the Forum in Rome, after a simple request of a photograph. It was the start of a friendship that included a visit to Finland and the Arctic Circle and a visit to India by Risto and his daughter Vanessa to attend Sidharth's wedding.

And, the story of an out of town/lost fellow Indian driving in circles, who stopped and asked for directions from Prakash, the 'gardener' pruning roses in his Edina garden. That led to an offer of tea, a long conversation and a lifelong friendship with Gopal Khanna.

Family

Prakash always dreamt of becoming a Physician. To his delight, that dream was fulfilled when both his sons obtained an MD/PhD from Harvard, after receiving undergraduate degrees from MIT.

Rishi, their youngest son completed his fellowship/research in oncology at Massachusetts General and is a Post Doc at Broad (pronounced Brode) Institute, a biomedical and genomic research center. He is married to Priya, an endocrinologist and the couple have blessed Prakash and Kamala with a three year old granddaughter and a baby grandson.

Sidharth, their oldest son, is the 'Chief of Head & Neck Surgery' in the Department of Otolaryngology-Head & Neck Surgery, at Washington University in St.Louis, and has specialized in micro vascular reconstructive surgery. His wife Akshita is an MBA from MIT Sloan, currently working as a Director of Digital Marketing at Enterprise, Inc. They have three young daughters.

Prakash with Family

They are the main reason Prakash and Kamala moved to St.Louis in 2019, a big move for a self-professed "Edina Bigot".with Family

'Puram Motel' is as busy as ever in St. Louis, and always open for business. Prakash and Kamala live life fully in the present and take one day at a time. They enjoy the time spent with their sons and daughters-in-law, and adore their grandchildren.

And as their friend Mahesh wrote in the birthday book, Prakash continues to embody:

A Fullness of Light; Optimism so very Bright; Engaging and Caring; Friendships ever enduring; Such versatility in your personality; We all laud in unanimity; Success

Under the Banyan Tree

in many dimensions; Paths paved without apprehensions; A rich life you have been leading; A warm family so supporting!

A poem by Mahesh Kanumury

CHAPTER 14

MY LITTLE FIGHTER

This is the heartwarming saga of Rijuta Pathre, and her 43 year quest, to give her daughter and other children born with severe mental and physical disabilities, a life that all children enjoy.

"I see a young bud blooming into a new personality. She is not the unreachable soul with a twisted body. She is in contact with the world and with emotions, fear and love".

Rijuta and Sadanand Pathre's second daughter Meenakshi, affectionately known as Minu was born in 1979. From the early age of 2 months, it became evident that Minu had significant disabilities that left her unable to speak, and engage in activities like crawl, see and move. At the age of five months, after undergoing a battery of tests, a doctor at the University of Minnesota, told them that Minu would not see her first birthday: *"The parents should put her in an institution and forget she was born. She is not going to amount to anything"*. These words seared her consciousness like a branding iron!

Three years ago, Rijuta and her family celebrated Minu's 40th birthday!

"Everybody's life has importance, no matter what their ability is. Minu is dependent on other people's care, but she has such stubbornness and will power that she gets things done in the way she wants. So she has power over her life. She cries, she has facial expressions that convey her desires, and then she has that big smile that makes everything worthwhile".

Family Life

Rijuta came to the US in 1970, soon after her marriage to Sadanand. The culture and lifestyle were new and strange, but she assimilated, catering to her passion for Indian home cooking with improvised ingredients, viewing Bollywood movies at the Bell Museum and meeting other young Indian couples. She became one of the founding members of the Marathi Association of Minnesota, and the Bharat School which later evolved to SILC (School of Indian Languages and Culture). Rijuta also became involved in the community, organizing cultural programs from dramas to children's dances, and flexed her writing skills by penning skits. She recalls these times as some of her *"most fun days"*, struggling for money, but deriving great pleasure from a shared ice cream cone with her husband (a Ph.D student in chemistry at the University of Minnesota) bought from a leftover laundry quarter.

Their eldest daughter Anviksha was born in

1974. She is a successful Psychologist with two practices in Chicago. Happily married, she has blessed Rijuta and Sadanand with two teenage grandchildren, aged 14 and 11.

The strong bond between five year old Anviksha and Minu was fostered from the time Minu was born. Anviksha was made to feel an integral part of Minu's care team. She even insisted that Minu be her First Grade 'Show and Tell' project, her story focusing on: 'Our love for her; How cute she is; How we care for her'.

146

Under the Banyan Tree

Meenakshi (Minu) was born in 1979 and labeled 'severely' impaired, without a specific diagnosis. Prognosis was dim without much hope for the future. Ignoring professional advice to institutionalize her, they brought her home to love and nurture.

For 11 years, Rijuta took care of Minu alone while Sadanand supported the family as a chemist at 3M. Minu was enrolled in an infant stimulation program, then she went to a Developmental Achievement Center (DAC), and finally to the public school's multi-handicapped unit. The teachers were wonderful and the family received a lot of support, but it did not move Minu upward.

Just about then their prayers were answered. They were able to enroll in 'A chance to Grow', a Sandler Brown Program. The first six months were hard and demanding, yet gratifying. With an army of volunteers that included family, friends and 21 parishioners from the Blessed Virgin Mary Church in Maplewood, Minu was attended to 6-7 hours a day. The positive changes included weight gain, fewer illnesses and even a crawling pattern on the floor.

Unfortunately, after 4 years and a home move, they had to discontinue the program as they lost most of their volunteers, but key positive changes stayed that included: normal light reflexes and tracking people and objects; *"she*

*is aware of her surroundings; understands
language; and can even throw temper
tantrums".*

Partners In Policymaking

Around that time, Rijuta joined a two year
leadership training program for parents of
children with disability: Partners in
Policymaking. *"When I graduated I was so
empowered. It changed me inside out. I
became a fierce advocate not only for my
daughter but for all people with disability".*

A summer workshop provided new skills such
as writing and reviewing grants. Rijuta was also
selected to serve on their Rule Advisory
Committee, and became part of a study group
to implement legislative changes. It gave her
direction, a new path to march on and
appreciate life as a precious and divine asset.

*"It enlightened me to get actively involved in
different organizations, to voice my concerns,
work on changing laws, become part of a task
force at the state level on information
dissemination at doctor's offices, reaching
health and social workers and affected
parents".*

Rijuta also sat on many Governor's advisory
councils and was a board member of the
'Special Education Advisory Council'.

Minu Enjoying Life

*"I never would have imagined my daughter
taking horseback rides or going to Disney
World. Minu goes camping, for a walk in the
woods with us, and to Anviksha's dance
recitals. We take her to the mall and out for*

*lunches and dinners, where
she sees her friends and kids
from school, and all the kids
who have known her don't
think anything different
about her".*

After traveling to
memorable places like England, India,
Yellowstone, Grand Canyon and California as a
family, they discovered camping. Minu joined
them on all their camping trips.

Rijuta wrote a prize winning article for the St
Paul Sunday Pioneer Press, of their trip to
Itasca National Park, genesis of the mighty
Mississippi river. Preparing for every
emergency, their gear could have taken them to
the North Pole!

*"We felt such a closeness that nothing else
seemed to exist. Open space with a blanket of
sky full of stars. Our family seemed to be
closer than before. We laughed, watched birds
and made sandcastles. Now we go camping*

whether it rains or shines. We love every minute of it".

As Life Moves On

Rijuta and Sadanand are now in their mid-seventies and live with many health challenges. The Covid pandemic has affected their care of Minu. Federal and State programs have been cut back and/or discontinued. Their need for caregivers is acute, as they struggle alone to care for their 43 year old daughter. Any referrals for qualified caregivers are appreciated and can be sent to 'randspathre@gmail.com'.

With all the challenges they have faced and continue to, Rijuta and Sadanand have never lost their positive attitude and have a tremendous zest for life. The love of friends and family and good food keep them smiling. Rijuta's friends call her 'Dear Abby' since she has a solution to every psychological dilemma. They entertain and are entertained frequently: birthdays, baby showers, weddings, Indian festivals such as 'Diwali' and 'Kojagiri Purnima' celebrated with a boat ride on Lake Minnetonka, and Christmas parties.

"I represent a neglected minority population. I am a voice for those who don't have a voice in this political environment. My life has been enriched by my daughter and family. I was able to spread my wings to see the world at different angles, which I would otherwise never have seen. My mind still thinks I am only 25".

Rijuta And Her Family Support Group

CHAPTER 15

YUM YUM YUM

U nder the banner of AshaUSA, and in keeping with its mission of health and harmony, the 'Hum Group' program, supported generously by the Dr. Dash Foundation was launched in August 2015. It was ideated by residents of the local community, as an arena for seniors to socialize and form friendships, especially important for new seniors to the US, and parents

visiting their adult children for a few months of the year. The first event was held at the home of AshaUSA's founder Kamala Puram with only five members. Since then it has grown exponentially with over 100 global seniors on its roster, and in-person events typically host 30-40. During covid, and the hardships brought about by enforced isolation and loneliness, the 'Hum Group' zoom meetings were a beacon of light and connection. Through songs, poetry, games, celebration of festivals and birthdays, hope and resilience prevailed.

Hum as the collective 'US' stands for 'H'=Hear Each Other, 'U'=Understand Each Other, 'M'= Mingle With Each Other.

The 'Hum Group' seniors are talented home chefs, and sampling their delicious 'potluck' creations has become a highlight of the themed monthly gatherings and once a year picnic.

The story below showcases the culinary skills of Asha USA's 'Hum Group' members.

Usha Katyal's Sprouts Salad

Usha is one of the founding members of Hum Group. She moved to the US in 2001 from Ahmedabad, soon after the devastating earthquake in the Western State of Gujarat. Since 2004 she has lived in the Twin Cities area. Starting as a substitute Recreation Leader in 2004 in the Edina School system, she worked for 15 years, before the onset of Covid caused her to leave. She lives with her son and his family, and has another daughter in India. She is blessed with 5 grandchildren.

Sprouts Salad Recipe

Ingredients: 2 Cups of sprouted green mung; 1 cucumber; 1 Tomato; 1/3 cup red or white onion; 2 green spring onion; 1 carrot; 2 red radish; 1 celery stalk; 1/2 cup cabbage; 1/3 cup red/yellow bell pepper; 2-3 sprigs mint; 2/3 tbsp lemon juice; 1 tbsp chopped cilantro; 1 tsp each of chaat masala, coarse pepper and roasted ground cumin; salt to taste.

Preparation: Put the sprouts in a bowl; add finely chopped vegetables to the sprouts; add lemon juice and all the spices and mix well (can add chopped green chilies or red chili powder for extra oomph!).

Asha Srivastava's Naryal Ki Barfee (Coconut Sweet)

Asha and her husband Prem immigrated to the US in 1998 after Prem retired from government service in India. The incentive for coming to the US was the birth of their granddaughter. As a self taught artist, Asha creates arts and crafts in many mediums, including cooking, constantly innovating new methods. They have two daughters and three granddaughters and live in the Twin Cities area.

Coconut Barfi Recipe

*Ingredients:*70 gms sugar; 1/4 cup water; 2 tbsp milk; 75 gms coconut powder; 50 gms dried mawa powder; 1/2 tsp green elaichi powder; 2 drops rose essence; pistachio or almond flakes.

Preparation: Put sugar and water in pan and bring to boil; add 2 tbsp milk; lower the heat and add coconut and mawa powder, mix well to form a dry clumpy mix; take off the heat and mix in elaichi powder and rose essence; grease a plate with butter or ghee and spread the mix in a square shape 1/4 inch thick; using a wet spatula smooth and pat down with a light touch; sprinkle pistachio/almond garnish, pressing in with a wet spatula; let it cool and rest; cut into diamond shapes with spatula/sharp knife.

Urmila Madhok's Butterscotch Delight

Urmila Madhok moved to Minnesota after 36 years teaching math at Minot State University in Minot, ND. Urmila has two children, a son and a daughter and one granddaughter. She is a talented craftsperson and is fond of sewing, making all her own clothes. She also likes to cook and create her own recipes.

Butterscotch Delight Recipe

Ingredients: 1 stick butter; 1 cup flour; 1/3 cup chopped walnuts; 1 cup powdered sugar; 8 oz package cream cheese; 8 oz container cool whip; 3 oz package each of instant vanilla and instant butterscotch pudding; 1/4 cup toasted coconut; 3 cups milk.

Preparation: Mix butter and flour with electric hand mixer; stir in walnuts; press into a 9×13 greased glass bowl; bake in a preheated oven at 375 degrees for 10-15 minutes; let it cool; mix powdered sugar and cream cheese with an electric hand mixer in a mixing bowl; add half the cool whip stirring well and spread evenly on cooled crust; mix vanilla and butterscotch puddings in a mixing bowl; gradually add milk to pudding using electric hand mixer until it thickens; spread on the second layer of cool whip evenly; finally spread the remaining half cool whip and sprinkle the toasted coconut on the cool whip; refrigerate overnight; serve after cutting into desired pieces.

Sarla Arora's Dahi Baray

Sarla Arora recently aced her US citizenship test after moving to Minnesota 6-7 years ago. She lives with her only son and his family in the

Twin Cities area. She is a valued member of her community and gives piano recitals twice a year. Sarla also composes beautiful poetry. She loves to knit and sew and her cooking skills are enjoyed by her twin teenage grandsons and at many parties hosted at home.

Dahi Baray Recipe

Ingredients: I cup each split moong daal beans and split Urad daal lentils without skin; 1/4 cup fenugreek seeds or methi dana; 3-4 cups of plain yogurt; roasted cumin, black peppercorn and red chili powders; salt, tamarind and date chutney and mint leaves for garnish per taste.

Preparation: Soak lentils overnight for 10-12 hours separately; soak fenugreek seeds with one of the lentils; finely grind each lentil separately; mix ground lentils together and mix well till the mixture gets fluffy; test a small drop of mixture in cup of water: well whisked mixture will float to the top; heat oil in a pan and lightly fry the mixture in small balls; do not deep fry, balls should be yellow-light brown in color; add the fried balls to hot water (should not be boiling) and soak for 30 minutes; lightly squeeze the soaked balls and add to cold tap water; add yogurt to a bowl and whisk well; remove half of the whisked yogurt and set aside; add mint leaves to remaining yogurt; squeeze the soaked balls lightly and add to yogurt with mint leaves; garnish with red chili, peppercorn, roasted cumin powders and salt; add the remaining yogurt till the balls are covered; add tamarind and date chutney and serve cold (Extra balls can be frozen for later use).

Jayshree Desai's Pedhas

Jayshree and Bihari Desai were married in 1974 and she arrived in Chicago to join Bihari in 1975, in the midst of a raging blizzard. It was an 'exciting' introduction to her life in the US. In 1987 after obtaining a second BS in Chemical Engineering, she retired from Xcel Energy after 22 years. She spends her time helping STEM school students and also mentors University of Minnesota engineering students and the Society of Women Engineers. She enjoys playing bridge, and visiting her kids' families. She has a doctor son and a lawyer daughter and 4 grandchildren.

Pedhas Recipe

Ingredients: 1 small can of Sweetened condensed milk; 1.5 stick of unsalted butter; 100-150 ml milk; 1-2 cups instant dry milk carnation powder; cardamom powder; 2-3 tbsp sugar; saffron for taste and color; shelled or unshelled almonds; one butter coated pan.

Preparation: Melt butter stick; add condensed milk can; mix well at low flame; add milk and sugar and keep mixing at low flame; add cardamom powder and saffron; add carnation powder and mix till it does not stick to the spoon; roll pedas and cool in butter coated pan; garnish with almonds.

Bharati Mehta's Mini Uttapam

 Bharati and Rajnikant moved to the US in 1975 to work in the medical profession, first in Massachusetts, then New York, and for 36 years in Minot, North Dakota. After retirement they moved to the Twin Cities area to be closer to their children. They are proud of their 3 children and 2 grandchildren, and keep active by volunteering for the non-profit group 'Sewa' and the Hindu Temple.

Mini Uttapam Recipe

Ingredients: 2 cups rice; 1 cup urad daal; 1/2 cup sooji; 1 tsp methi seeds; diced onion and tomatoes, salt, ginger and green chilies per taste.

Preparation: Soak rice, daal and methi seeds separately for 12 hours; grind each separately; mix everything in big bowl with sooji (cream of wheat); ferment mixture for 8-12 hours; add salt, ginger, chilies and diced onion and tomatoes; use mini pancake pan to make uttapam by ladling mix into mold; serve with tamarind and coriander chutneys.

Kiran Manchanda's Sabu Dana Vada

Kiran is a retired post graduate chemistry teacher. She loves being a member of the Hum Parivar. She has a great passion for travel and

wanders tirelessly between her daughter's home in the Twin Cities and her son in San Francisco. She also has a strong passion for music and during Covid, she pursued singing. She is the proud grandmother of 4. She loves socializing and cooking.

Sabu Dana Vada Recipe

Ingredients: 1/2 cup sabu dana; 1 heaped cup medium sized cubed potatoes; 1/4 cup peanuts; 1 tbsp chopped coriander leaves; 1/2 tsp cumin seeds; 2 green chilies; 1/3 tsp salt per taste; 11/2 tsp lemon juice.

Preparation: Soak washed sabu dana overnight and check that they are not hard inside in the morning; crush soaked sabu dana; grind roasted peanuts; boil and peel and mash potatoes; mix crushed sabudana, potatoes, peanut powder, chopped green chilies, coriander, cumin, salt and lemon juice; make 10 to 12 balls, flatten them to make tikki/vada; heat oil in a kadai to medium flame; test one tikki in oil; if it breaks add 1 tsp flour and remake tikki after mixing well; fry tikki till golden brown and drain excess oil on paper towel; serve with green and red chutney.

Sudha Arora's Barfi

Sudha Arora started her married journey in the US in 1964. She spent most of her career in banking at Wells Fargo and US Bank. Sudha has one son and one daughter and 6 grandchildren She lives independently in a sun filled home in New Brighton, MN and her days are filled with family including her sisters who live in the area. She is a talented cook who quilts, and has won many competitions for her place mats and embroidered towels. (Though not a full fledged member of the Hum Group, Sudha keeps in close contact with many members).

Barfi Recipe

Ingredients: 1 15oz container of Ricotta cheese; 1/2 stick butter; 1 packet slivered skinned almonds ground to crumbs; 11/4 cup carnation dry milk.

Preparation: Melt butter in microwave; mix all ingredients in bowl with melted butter; cook for 21/2 minutes in microwave; mix; cook for another 21/2 minutes; mix; cook for another 21/2 minutes in microwave; (total microwave time 71/2 minutes); spread mix on buttered cookie sheet; after 10 minutes cut to desired size and shape.

Rifka Kaka's Black Masoor Pulau and Yogurt Curry

Rifka moved permanently to the US in 2004, though she was a frequent visitor since 1981. The Hum Meet's are a highlight for her and she enjoys the many friends she has made in the 'Hum Group'. She lives in the Twin Cities area with her daughter, your author, who loves being with her – to say nothing of the amazing cooking, and also has a son in Chicago. She is also the proud grandmother of two loving grandsons who visit her often. She loves to do jigsaw puzzles and read and watch movies and FaceTime with her sisters and extended family in India.

Black Masoor Pulau and Yogurt Curry Recipe

 *Ingredients:* 11/4 cup black masoor daal; 1 big chopped tomato and onion; 2 green chilis; 2 garlic pods; 4 cloves; 1 inch stick cinnamon; 4 curry leaves; salt per taste; 11/4 cup rice. *Yogurt Curry:* 1 cup plain yogurt; 2tbsp ground channa dal(besan); 1/4 tsp each fenugreek seeds and cumin seeds; 1/2 tsp mixed coriander/cumin powder; 4 curry leaves; 1 chopped tomato and 1/2 small onion; 2 green chilies; 1/2 tsp red chili powder; salt per taste.

Preparation: Soak Masoor in water for 2 hours; Boil till soft; Save masoor water and 2 tbsp boiled masoor for yogurt curry base; sauté garlic, curry leaves, cardamom, cloves, cumin till light brown; add chopped onions until light crispy brown; add tomatoes, green chilies and salt till well mixed; add boiled masoor to mix and cook for 10-15 minutes; cook rice in separate pan; add cooked masoor layer between two layers of cooked rice and do a final steam. *Yogurt Curry:* In a pan add masoor water and remaining boiled masoor to yogurt and besan/channa daal and mix to create a soft paste; in a separate pan sauté onion, garlic, cumin; methi and curry leaves; add red chili powder and coriander/cumin powder and turmeric and sauté for 1 minute; add tomatoes and salt and yogurt mix (with extra water if needed for consistency) and cook till oil separates and floats to the top.

Nirmal Bhardwaj's Namak Paare

Nirmal and Suresh Bhardwaj moved to the US in 1970 and 1974 respectively, and journeyed across the US before settling in Minneapolis in 2016 to be closer to their son and his family. Nirmal spent 17 years in a banking career and volunteered to teach Hindi at a community college in Ohio. They have 2 sons and 4 grandchildren and enjoy the beauty of Minnesota's Cedar Lake from their beautiful home.

Namak Paare Recipe

Ingredients: 5 cups all purpose flour; 2 tsp salt; 11/2 tsp ajwain(carom seeds); 3/4 cup plus more for deep frying; water to make dough.

Preparation: Mix flour, salt and ajwain well in a large bowl; add oil and mix well; add water slowly to make a dough; dough should be little harder than chapati dough; cover the dough and let rest for 1/2 hr; make balls and roll like chapati; cut rolled dough in diamond shapes; deep fry till golden brown.

Santosh Jhanjee's Feast Of Delights

Santosh Jhanjee is an erudite published poet of evocative Hindi poems of meaningful beauty. Santosh came to the US in 1985 with her husband and two teenage sons and $20 in her pocket. Today she lives an independent life on her own terms, surrounded by many friends and a loving family that includes 2 doctor sons, 4 grandchildren and sisters. As an accomplished cook, her feast of delights features 3 of her favorite recipes: Mathri, Halwa and Daal Paratha.

Mathri Recipe

Ingredients: 3 cups all purpose flour; 2 cups atta; 1 cup rice flour; 1 cup oil; pinch of baking soda; 2 tsp each ajwain and coarse black ground pepper; 1 tsp each cumin seeds and salt; water for dough.

Preparation: Mix all the dry ingredients well; add oil and mix well; add water slowly to make dough (should be harder than poori dough); make small 1/2 inch thick flattened balls with a rolling pin; pierce few holes in dough to prevent puffing while deep frying in medium heat till golden brown; enjoy with pickle and chutney.

Halwa Recipe

Ingredients: 1 stick unsalted butter; 1/2 cup cream of wheat; 1/4 cup each coarse ground chickpea flour and ground cracked wheat; 1 cup sugar; 5 cups water; chopped nuts of choice; 1/2 tsp cardamom; 1 tbsp dried milk.

Preparation: Melt butter in pan; add cream of wheat, chickpea flour, cracked wheat and brown the mix in butter; using 2nd pan melt sugar and cardamom in water; also add water to dry ingredients and stir the mix till it thickens without sticking to the pan; turn off gas; add dried milk and mix in well; garnish with choice of nuts and cardamom.

Daal Paratha Recipe For Leftovers

Ingredients: Leftover daal or vegetables; (following ingredients quantities based on leftovers) chopped spinach, mint, green chilies, ajwain, jeera, red chili flakes, oil, salt per taste, butter for garnish.

Santosh's Mathri, Halwa and Daal Paratha

Preparation: Mix all the ingredients together and make into a soft, pliable dough; water may not be required as cooked leftovers may have water; add water if needed; add 1 tbsp of oil;

divide the dough into equal parts and roll into a
ball; flatten the ball and roll into desired shape
i.e. square, round; on medium to hot griddle
cook evenly on both sides; garnish with butter
and serve with pickle and raita.

CHAPTER 16

"I'M PAID TO GO FISHING EVERYDAY..."

D
r. Asgi Fazleabas, is the University Distinguished Professor at Michigan State University, and a renowned expert in female reproduction.

Asgi is recognized world-wide for his outstanding contributions to 'Women's Health'. His service to the scientific world has been most significant through his research, major leadership positions in scientific communities, serving on 'Federal Grant Review' panels, and a frequent recipient of 'National Institute of Health (NIH)' grants. Asgi may be a passionate scientist with an illustrious career, but he has his priorities set right. As he says time and again: *"The most important thing to me is my family, and most importantly my wife: who is my anchor; my best friend; and my companion; who keeps me on the straight and narrow, and our two kids. Papers get rejected, grants get rejected, but you go home and you get a hug, and everything is all great".*

Early Years

Asgi grew up in Columbo, in the beautiful country of Sri Lanka. His father was a leading 'Ear, Nose and Throat' surgeon and both him and his mother instilled the value of education from an early age.

His father hoped Asgi would follow in his footsteps, but Asgi had a thirst for 'new' and 'different': *"I did not want to be pigeonholed into an area of specialization, so I ended up deciding that a career in science would be more fun than going to medical school"*.

He became interested in reproductive biology in 8th grade, at St. Thomas boarding school, located in the beautiful Highlands of Sri Lanka. His responsibilities on the school farm included monitoring the incubator, where chicken eggs were laid to hatch. He was fascinated by the rapid pace of blood vessel development, and detecting a heartbeat within a few days. The more he learned about fertilization and early embryo development, the more *"hooked"* he was on reproductive biology.

Arrival In The US

After three years of undergrad studies in Sri Lanka, he arrived in the US to finish that degree in 1974. This was followed by an impressive academic resume: a graduate degree in 1976; a PH.D in 1980; and postdoctoral training in 1983. As a full Professor by 1995, his impact on students continues to resound today, in the hallways of countless Universities and Hospitals. In 2009, he joined Michigan State University (after 26 years at the University of Illinois, Chicago) as  the Professor and Associate Chair of Research in the Department of Obstetrics, Gynecology and Reproductive Biology, Director of the Center for Women's Health Research, and Co-Director of the Reproductive and Developmental Sciences Program. This move was the culmination of an impressive career, with breakthrough achievements and key discoveries in 'Women's Health'. These have significantly helped women dealing with infertility, and provided hope for Endometriosis, an enigmatic disease that affects over 175 million reproductive aged women worldwide.

Family Life

Asgi married Sherebanu in December 2001, after a long acquaintance, and reconnection in 2020. This was the beginning of the happiest years of Asgi's life. The marriage has resulted in a thriving partnership, producing two beautiful children and travel adventures in over 90+ countries.

Asgi and Sherebanu's union has resulted in an exciting career for Sherebanu. As President, she established her award winning boutique travel company, A&S Signature Journeys, soon after their marriage in 2001. She offers 30 years of experience to travel agents in the U.S. market, building customized vacations that are rich in history, culture and culinary explorations. Her enthusiasm for travel has led her to every corner of the globe, in search of exhilarating destinations, often accompanied by Asgi and later their children.

Admirably, the tours are designed to give back

Gorillas in Rwanda

to local communities and conservation projects. One such project is the Faith Foundation in Rwanda. Clients visit the school located in a small village by the Ruhengiri mountains, whose main source of income comes from the Gorilla Safaris. Faith Foundation supports the children in the area with meals, education and jobs.

A new project is the 'Mara Meeru' Cheetah Conservation Center, in the Mara in Kenya.

The Scientist

For all his achievements, Asgi is a humble man!

His breakthrough work for the past 25 years, utilizing the 'Baboon' as a non-human primate model, has allowed for significant discoveries and applications towards endometriosis, fertility treatments and pregnancy in humans.

He is widely known as the consummate collaborator and has readily shared his research findings, and biological specimens with scientists around the world. He has also presented at over 240 invited talks globally. Not only has he published over 200 scholarly works in prestigious journals, but his laboratory is an intellectually stimulating training ground for undergraduate, graduate and medical students, postdoctoral fellows and visiting scientists.

He is the recipient of over 25 prestigious awards, in recognition of his significant contributions to the improvement of women's lives and health. The award that means the most to him came in November 2023, from his home country of Sri Lanka. He is one of 6 winners of the 2022 Sri Lanka Foundation 'Lifetime Achievement Award'. Awards are given to individuals for 'extraordinary' achievement, who have impacted the quality of life of Sri Lankans in the US and around the world, and made 'Mother Lanka proud'.

University of Illinois Alumni Career Achievement Award

This brings full circle the fulfilling journey of a 13 year old boy, who discovered his life's vocation, 'candling' chicks in an incubator, over 55 years ago in the Highlands of Sri Lanka.

"My parents instilled in me from a very young age that when you are more fortunate than others, you have to give back. Being of service to the community and fellow human beings is an important aspect of being an individual. This upbringing has carried over into my career. Being able to serve the scientific community that nourishes and sustains me, means being involved in advocacy for reproductive rights, and training the next generation of scientists".

CHAPTER 17

HOW MY NERVOUS SYSTEM BECAME MY CUP OF TEA

Niloufer Merchant, a Minnesota resident of thirty-one years is an activist and advocate for underserved populations.

TEDx St Cloud, October 14, 2021

Niloufer reached a significant milestone in her multifaceted life journey, when she gave a Tedx Talk to an audience of 500+. This journey began in British Aden, and flourishes in the Twin Cities today.

Niloufer was invited to present at Tedx by the 'St.Cloud' Tedx committee, a city that has benefited from her generous contributions for 28+ years. She was one of a distinguished line-up of nine luminaries, ranging from a Physicist to a Robotics expert to the President of a University.

The theme of this year's event was 'Embrace', giving the audience an opportunity to consider new ideas, and address together the challenges faced as individuals and as a community.

In her Tedx talk, Niloufer highlighted *"how emerging theories in neuroscience validate ancient practices. These practices help our nervous systems feel regulated, when we feel safe and socially connected with others"*. Niloufer compared the simple practice of drinking tea together in the Indian culture, as a parallel to co-regulating with others.

The Tedx presentation was an affirmation of Niloufer's life's commitment and work, and the video can be viewed on YouTube:*https://youtu.be/T-NQToC9iKM*

Tracing Her Multi-Cultural Identity

"As I look back, I see a kaleidoscope of multicultural experiences that have shaped my life".

Niloufer was born in the city of Aden, a seaport in Yemen and a British Colony at the time, to hardworking, entrepreneurial parents. Her earliest memories include a mixture of happy-go-lucky days, playing on the sandy beaches of the Red Sea with her siblings. The family lived in the part of the city that was located inside an extinct volcanic crater, providing endless fascination to a young child. Her fondest recollections are of her smiling mother, and the unconditional love she showered on her family. She was the role model in Niloufer's own parenting journey and her wisdom guides her every day: *"She inspired us to be our best selves in every way"*.

As the political power shifted from the British to the Yemeni, sounds of gunfire and civil unrest prompted her parents to send Niloufer and her sister to boarding school in Pune, India for safety and a better education.

The school run by British Anglican nuns was run on strict christian principles, bringing more cultural transition to the eight year old Niloufer, after immersion in the Arab culture of Aden. Niloufer reminisces that her experiences were parallel to the beloved British children book series, 'Mallory Towers' by Enid Blyton, involving midnight feasts and other escapades.

In Pune, Niloufer was raised and surrounded by a tight knit circle, while her parents were away in Aden. Extended family and the large 'Colony' of neighbors: Hindus, Christians, Jews and Muslims enveloped them in their 'Village', *"an extensive kinship network with many surrogate aunts and uncles"*. Every festival and religious holiday was celebrated with gusto.

Niloufer and her sister, surrounded by a loving, nurturing community, were cradled in a cocoon of security.

Coming To The US

*"Education was a very big thing for my dad".
Having come from humble beginnings, "he
was very keen that we would be able to
support ourselves".*

Niloufer's true passion lay in Psychology, but
she negotiated a compromise with her father
who wanted her to become a medical doctor. If
persevering at the sciences for two years was
not successful, she was free to pursue her own
'dream', which she eventually realized, with a
Graduate Masters in Psychology from the
University of Pune.

On impulse and at the urging of a friend, she
applied and was admitted, with a graduate
assistantship, to the University of Wisconsin-
Whitewater, and obtained her second Masters
in Counseling. But, not before she achieved a
life long degree in assimilation, small town
America, eurocentrism in course material and
racism.

Her next stop was the University of Cincinnati,
to pursue and complete a Doctorate in
Counseling. She finally had the 'Doctor' title
that her father had always wanted for his
daughter!

A pivotal turning point for Niloufer, which
influenced her future advocacy work, was her

participation in a racial awareness pilot project in Cincinnati. She was so fascinated and involved with this initiative that four years later she assumed Directorship of the program.

Around this time she was introduced to her future husband Moiz, born and raised in Mumbai and living in Texas. After a whirlwind courtship, they were married three months later in a traditional Indian wedding, replete with all the rituals of henna, gifts, colorful bridal wear and jewels.

Moiz and Niloufer successfully practiced family parenting. They shared the work of a household based upon skill, not gender. *"My partner does most of the cooking because he is a far better cook"*. In adjusting traditional gender roles, her husband supported her career and activism in the community, so Niloufer *"can go do her thing"*.

 Niloufer found the most satisfaction in her family life. Being the mother of two boys allowed her to experience *"the most esoteric peace work that exists"*. They grounded her, by making her focus on the simple realities: *"I'm hungry"; "Can you please*

help me with my homework"; "Can you play with me".
Her joy was boundless in 2021, when their eldest son got married in the United Kingdom, and Niloufer finally had a daughter.

ST. Cloud University – SCSU and Advocacy

Niloufer moved to St. Cloud, to take a position as Assistant Professor of Applied Psychology at St.Cloud State University in 1991, retiring twenty-eight years later as Professor Emeritus, Clinical Mental Health Counseling, Graduate program.

It was a tumultuous time at SCSU with disharmony and unrest. Niloufer worked to bring conflicting sides together and assumed the Co-Chair of the 'Faculty and Staff of Color Caucus' for seven years. She held many leadership positions on campus over a thirty year period, including Department Chair.

A key to her classroom success was showing her humanity to her students: *"I might cry with them, be upset about things. I disclose my own struggles and perspectives on the issues".*

Multiculturalism, a binding thread through her entire life, was at the core of her teaching courses. Using an experiential approach on tough issues empowered her students, by taking them on a self-awareness journey. A confrontation of diverse perspectives, finally led them to a realization that they were part of the solution.

Being employed at SCSU University engaged Niloufer in the broader community. She participated in a community diversity task force for the Mayor of St. Cloud, and also served as Interim Director of the SCSU Women's Center. It was a very fulfilling role for Niloufer, as the mission was to promote women, and respond to issues affecting women on campus and in society.

Niloufer's devotion to advocacy, and empowerment of knowledge and wellness in underserved populations remained inexhaustible. She was a co-founder of 'Parents of Children of Color and Concerned Citizens', and assumed other influential positions in the St.Cloud Community and professional organizations locally and nationally.
At any point she was involved in seven or eight projects, in addition to her teaching responsibilities.

Complexity Of Identities

As Niloufer's time in her adoptive country lengthened, she straddled two, three and four worlds. She dressed, ate, spoke and behaved differently when she was at home versus work, and within her conservative and traditional religious community. She saw herself as a radical feminist in one context and wearing traditional garb and following conservative values in another.

Over the years, she has seen this complex reality in a new light. *"Cultural identity is not static or one-dimensional. It is multi-dimensional and contextual"*.

She is true to herself *"in all places, just showing different facets of myself depending on where I am. I have begun to appreciate the beauty of living in multiple worlds. I now embrace the complexity of my identities and I am working on finding the common threads that bind us all"*

Gardening And Relaxing

Gardening has been a solace for her. The garden that Niloufer cultivated in her St.Cloud home helped balance the complexities of her life. She also loves to travel, exploring different culinary experiences, knitting and crocheting.

The Next Chapter

Retirement has proven elusive for Niloufer. After moving to the Twin Cities from St.Cloud four years ago, her husband's fervent wish was to spend their retirement years traveling, discovering the bounty of ethnic food in their new environment and spending quality time together.

However, Covid has disrupted many of those dreams. Also, Niloufer's relentless drive has led her down a different path.

Using the advanced training she had done in trauma related work, and her earlier involvement with 'Lutheran Social Services' and the 'Veterans Resilience Project', Niloufer set up her own successful practice as a Psychologist, specializing in emotional and relationship issues, PTSD, meditation and mindfulness.

Moiz runs the business side of the practice and was able to fulfill one of 'his' key retirement goals: Spending quality time with his wife!!

360 Degrees

"Education was a very big thing for my dad". He believed that a good education would enable 'us to stand on our own two feet'.

A young Niloufer with her Parents and Siblings

Inculcated in this theory from an early childhood, Niloufer's life journey has proven the veracity of her father's value system.

CHAPTER 18

'ONE DOESN'T NEED FEET, BUT COURAGE TO FLY HIGH'

Santosh Jhanjee's inspiring journey of courage and firm resolve is aptly illustrated by her own words:

"When Goals are alive, the land feels like open sky"

"One Doesn't need feet, but courage to fly high"

Santosh grew up in a traditional household in New Delhi, India and after an arranged marriage in 1968, and subsequent births of her two sons, happily fulfilled the roles of supportive wife and devoted mother.

Santosh gloried in everyday married life, celebrating festivals, and marking important milestones in her children's lives such as the Mundana, the eighth of the Hindu Samskaras (purification ceremony) in which a child receives their first haircut.

American Story

Her American story began in 1985, as an immigrant to the US, when she arrived at her sister's home in the Twin Cities, accompanied by her husband, two teenage sons, a heart full of confidence and firm resolve, and $20 in her purse!

Unlike many members of her family, Santosh had never desired a life in the US. However, when fate intervened, she felt tremendously blessed that she could give her sons the chance to pursue a different kind of success, in the country she had often heard referred to as the 'land of opportunity'. For her boys, she was determined to pursue this dream at any cost.

And thirty-seven years later, it has turned out to be a fulfilling life with many highs and lows and bitter-sweet moments.

On the first day of arrival, the family dropped their luggage at her sister's place, and immediately hit the streets to find employment. Though a large extended family offered assistance, her Indian upbringing would not allow her to accept help or be dependent on anybody.

"We had all decided that whatever work we can get, we will take it".

Their perseverance paid off and soon her husband and older son, just 16, were working as dishwashers at Dayton's and Scarpelli's restaurants respectively. Their 15 year old also got an hourly job and life moved slowly on, with the kids going to school during the day and working at night. Three months after setting foot on American soil, they had earned enough to feel financially independent, and moved from her sister's home to subsidized living. As soon as Santosh discovered a 'Children's Home Society Daycare' in her housing complex, she secured employment, first, as an hourly on-call worker, with full time status soon after.

As the years went by, Santosh felt that though *"life was picking up speed"*, the pace was not fast enough for her. Her boys were at the University of Minnesota on full scholarships and her husband was working for the government in a good job. But, to Santosh *"the destination was not even close yet"*.

She wanted more for herself!

And, with ingenuity and determination she got it! Her younger son was wrapping up a summer job at Fairview Hospital's corporate office and Santosh visualized taking his place when the summer was over.

This was a bold dream as everything, including the language was foreign to her. Apprehensive at first, she asked for and interviewed for his job. It was a courageous move but it paid off.

The work environment was new and strange at first: the phone system; unknown people; american english; transportation issues. Minnesota winters also presented a huge challenge. Commuting to work involved two bus connections, especially difficult in snow and thunderstorms. Slipping on icy streets resulted in broken bones but *"once I reached the office, I did not get up from my desk, even for lunch break or any other break"*.

As time flew by, her confidence knew no bounds. Hard work, commitment and honesty resulted in promotions every six months. Her Supervisor Kim, and Director Judy became her staunchest supporters. Santosh's joy was boundless when she received the 'Best Employee Award' in 1991. Santosh worked at Fairview for 25 years and finally took retirement in 2010, as a fractured foot made her commute to work difficult, and she wanted to *"enjoy life on her terms"*.

Today, Santosh lives an independent life of peace and happiness. Though she insists on living alone after her husband passed away in 1999, she gets great solace from her daily meditations and prayers, family and close friends. She is a gracious and welcoming hostess, serving delicious homemade sweets and savories.

Poetry

Santosh is a brilliant poet. She is the author of hundreds of poems written in Hindi, and scores of lined paper journals and promotional paper pads are a tribute to the talent and beauty of her verse.

Tribute to her mother

She is up by 5am, and after her morning prayers, walks 8-10 miles a day in her apartment complex, mentally composing her beautiful verse. When she is back home 3 hours later, she pens her mental compositions on one of the countless paper journals readily available.

Family

Her two sons have more than fulfilled Santosh's hopes, dreams and ambitions. They are happily married to women from India and have blessed her with four grandchildren. At her grandson's Mundana ceremony in 2001, the occasion evoked happy memories from her own son's Mundana in India 29 years ago.

Her younger son Rajat, is a cardiologist in Atlanta. He started his career as an electrical engineer with undergraduate and graduate degrees from the University of Minnesota and UCLA, before enrolling in the University of Minnesota Medical school. He is the recipient of prestigious scholarships, and combines his engineering and medical skills towards cardiovascular applications.

Her older son Rajan, lives in the Twin Cities area and is an Orthopedic Surgeon. His

background also includes degrees in electrical engineering with an emphasis on biomedical engineering from the University of Minnesota. He too is the recipient of many scholarships, and utilizes his engineering background in pioneering orthopedic applications.

American Dream

Today, Santosh lives the American dream surrounded by a broad and extremely close knit network of family and friends, including her sisters whom she sees every week. She attributes her own family's success to the tremendous support she received from her extended clan in the US, from the day she arrived at her sister's home in 1985, "without which we would not have been able to survive here".

Santosh with Sisters

CHAPTER 19

SEVEN RIVERS TO TEN THOUSAND LAKES

The versatile Preeti Mathur is a longtime Twin Cities resident, and an active member of the Indian American community.

THE BOOK

Preeti's crowning achievement in a career spanning many years as an Instructional Design and Technical Communication consultant, to now a freelance writer for her local paper the Shoreview Press, is the publication of her book 'From Seven Rivers to Ten Thousand Lakes'.

She was invited by the Minnesota Historical Society to write the book, after participation on the advisory committee that localized 'Beyond Bollywood', a Smithsonian exhibit in 2016.

Through personal stories and vivid photographs, the book offers an overview of the more than 40,000 people of Indian descent residing in Minnesota. It presents their pursuit and celebration of cultural and religious traditions, and the professional, political and economic contributions to their adopted state and country. Profiles of prominent individuals, businesses and organizations who form the cornerstone of the Indian American community in Minnesota round out the narrative.

Preeti's hope is that the book's stories told through the eyes and voices of the Indian American community will *"bring down the walls and divisions created today about people and views that are different from your own"*.

The book is available through Amazon and the Minnesota Historical Society:

https://www.amazon.com/Seven-Rivers-Ten-Thousand-Lakes/dp/168134114X/ref=cm_cr_arp_d_pl_foot_top?ie=UTF8.

https://shop.mnhs.org/products/seven-rivers-ten-thousand-lakes

ARRIVAL IN THE US

Preeti's story in the US began as a 21 year old bride, following a long distance two year courtship that kept the postal services busy between St. Paul and Hyderabad, India. As Preeti aptly summarized the years leading up to her nuptials, *"you can have an arranged marriage, but you cannot arrange your emotions"*.

Her husband first saw her at her maternal grandmother's home, when a marriage union brought their two families together. He claims that *"from the moment he saw Preeti, he knew he was going to marry her"*.

Preeti and her family would visit her grandmother's home 'Charminar' during the muslim festival of Muharram. In the annual 10th day procession, the elephant carrying the

Bibi-Ka-Alam (holy relic), would stop and collect the 'Offerings' from the windows of their respective grandmother's homes.

Forty years later the romance continues, and the story of their courtship is memorialized in a painting by Preeti.

Preeti's pictorial reconstruction of courtship during Bibi-Ka-Alam

SERIAL VOLUNTEER

Preeti's family and friends have affectionately titled her a 'Serial Volunteer'.

Soon after arriving in Minnesota in 1978, Preeti started her long commitment to SILC (School of India for Languages and Culture). *"SILC was an integral and very important part of my life here. I met so many like-minded people who have become life-long friends".*
Preeti joined SILC's predecessor Bharat School the year she arrived in the US, and became not only a founding member of SILC but its first treasurer. With no computers *"everything was recorded in a notebook".*

She was also the editor of the newsletter 'SILC Road' , a play on the Silk Road, the renowned route connecting China and the Far East to the Western World. The group found a resonance in the work they were doing through SILC, to the ancient route's lasting impact on Commerce, Culture and History. The SILC newsletters are now part of the Oral History project at the Minnesota History Center.

Over the course of an intense twenty year involvement, Preeti taught Hindi, Indian art, Pre-School, Culture Courses and served as Treasurer, Principal and President!!!

Following her father's voice of *"assimilating and giving back"* as a beacon, Preeti also dived wholeheartedly into volunteering at her kid's schools; scout troops; food drives; and soup kitchens. She was one of the first Indians to be nominated as an 'Associated Fellow' by her peers at the Society For Technical Communication on a national and international level.

CULTURAL AMBASSADOR

Through her work with SILC, she played the role of Cultural Ambassador during her early years in Minnesota. She saw her role as promoting and talking about Indian Culture. Preeti organized and arranged exhibits for the 'Festival of Nations', and publicized the festival on WCCO radio

As an IAM (India Association of Minnesota) board member she organized an Inter Faith prayer meeting at the State Capitol after 9-11, and gave presentations on India at various schools and organizations: Minneapolis Institute of Arts, MN Department of Transportation and Blue Cross/Blue Shield.

TRADITIONS

Rituals and traditions have always played an important role in South Asian families.

Under the Banyan Tree

Preeti's family tradition was inadvertently established from the realities and necessities of daily life.

"I made Khitchrie (a lentil rice dish) for dinner every Sunday. It started in the years when my Dad came to live with us after my mum passed away. He lived with us for 18 years and those were the busiest years of my life—working full-time with many deadlines, a husband who was always traveling, two active school-age kids and taking care of my Dad. So when it came to Sunday dinner, a one-pot meal like khitchrie worked well, especially since it appealed to both my Dad and the kids. I did not realize it had become a family tradition for my kids until my daughter, a new bride, called on a Sunday and told me she was making Khitchrie for her husband per our family tradition. I laughed so hard when I heard this".

Over the years, Preeti has extended her family Khitchrie tradition to provide succor for friends in need of comfort and recovering from illness. Her insistence to all and sundry to *'Eat Eat'*, has been an inherited influence from her mother. Her sister-in-law has fondly labeled her 'Annadata' or giver of food. As her son once commented *"my mum feeds kebabs even to the Geek Squad guys"*.

COMING FULL CIRCLE

As life comes full circle, it is all about the lessons that come from our parents. In honor of her dad and the influence he had over her own family during his eighteen years of living with them, Preeti dedicated her book 'From Seven Rivers to Ten Thousand Lakes' to her father Anand Mathur.

His parting advice when she left India in 1978 on her journey to Minnesota, was *"assimilate and adapt without giving up your values. Do community service; be proud of your culture and share it; but make sure you also learn from others"*.

"Daddy I hope I have made you proud".

CHAPTER 20

GARDENS: INSPIRATION AND REMEMBRANCE

N ot only is Vatsala Menon, a Master Gardener but a creative artist in her own right.

Vatsala grew up in a large combined family in Trivandrum in the southern state of Kerala, in the charmingly named house 'Anandalayam' meaning joyous abode. Great grandparents, grandparents, parents, uncles, aunts, siblings and cousins formed a wonderful web of love, knowledge and support for the first 25 years of her life, providing a strong foundation for her future home in the US.

Three pronged pine tree

Vatsala moved into her current home in the Twin Cities area when her boys were in kindergarten and preschool. What sold her on the house was a large backyard and a pine tree with a three pronged trunk. It reminded her of Lord Shiva and the Trishul or trident, one of the principal symbols of

Hinduism representing the three trinities of creation, preservation and destruction.

Years later, after many paradigm shifts in her career from corporate America to graduate studies and finally elementary grade teacher in the St. Paul inner city school system, Vatsala made many plans at retirement: Freedom to pursue hobbies, hang out with like minded friends and spend newfound freedom gardening.

Then 'Covid' happened! Covid stealthily moved into her life and robbed Vatsala of another kind of freedom. Not being able to see and hold her first granddaughter, her children and the companionship of sharing meals and laughter with close friends.

After weeks of trying to wrap her head around this disruptive phenomenon and shifting priorities, the first tendrils of resilience emerged and she set a new course of action into unknown territories.

Fulfilling her dad's dream that his children, educated in catholic schools, understand the 'Puranas', finally became a reality. As Vatsala listened to the interpretations of these ancient Hindu texts, she was enveloped by her dad's aura.

When the University of Minnesota offered a Master Gardener course, Vatsala immersed herself completely in photosynthesis, soil structure, plant propagation and all the many facets of successful gardening.

The results of which are on glorious display in

A Garden Collage

her magnificent garden.

Vatsala's inspiration was her mother. Having grown up in India in the monsoon rains and with a graduate degree in botany, she infused a deep love of nature in her daughter. Though all the flowers of the North American prairie fascinated her, it was the undemanding purple lilacs that won her mother's heart.

200

Under the Banyan Tree

When her mother passed away twenty five years ago friends gifted her with a lilac sapling. It still flourishes steadfast, having braved many harsh Minnesota winters.

Creating totem/peace poles for the garden depicting intricate Indian paintings resulted in works of art that were as surprising to the creator as they were to her family.

Vatsala's favorite Covid activity after gardening was post dinner walks in the neighborhood with her husband, through the changing seasons of a long Covid year: Connecting with neighbors; observing backyard games and barbecues; enjoying their constant new companion the night sky with its waxing and waning moon, blanket of stars, Mars and Saturn competing for attention, occasionally low dark swirly clouds bringing the promise of a snowstorm.

For Vatsala, it has been a year of reckoning, a time to pause and take stock of what is important. "I hope for a change, a change from excess to moderation, a change from 'me' to 'us'.

Under the Banyan Tree

Author Bio and Picture

R uby Anik has lived in the Twin Cities area of Minnesota since 1997.

Originally from Mumbai, India she attended a Jesuit Convent and college, where her love of reading and writing was fostered and encouraged. She moved to the US in 1981, and spent her first 17 years in Chicago.

Ruby's 30+ year career has been focused in the Branding, Marketing and Advertising disciplines. In Chicago, she worked for several large advertising conglomerates, helping clients with their customer outreach strategies, establishing strong brand connections and loyalty. After moving to the client side at Pillsbury, Ruby also worked at Best Buy Corporate as the Senior Vice President of Marketing Communications, and at JCPenney Corporate as the Senior Vice President of Brand Marketing. She also had a seat on JCPenney's Executive Board.
Global public speaking in motivational leadership, and teaching the value of brand development and advocacy, afforded the opportunity to present at conferences around the world, also spurring her interest in travel.

Ruby'a personal passion includes writing, and she has penned a travel blog called '*www.rubyroams.com*' for travel wanderers, with a curiosity and thirst for exploration.

Ruby began volunteering with AshaUSA in 2020, crafting a blog on South Asians who have immigrated to the US, bringing to life their stories of resilience and hope. To date, 20 stories have been published and range from an 8 year old boy to a medical scientist to an 84 year old grandmother. These stories are being compiled in a book, to celebrate AshaUSA's 10th anniversary in September, 2024.

The blog is published as :
www.desistoriesashausa.com

Made in the USA
Columbia, SC
19 November 2024

46962051R00113